John Greenleaf Whittier

Home Ballads and Poems

John Greenleaf Whittier

Home Ballads and Poems

ISBN/EAN: 9783744792806

Printed in Europe, USA, Canada, Australia, Japan

Cover: Foto ©Thomas Meinert / pixelio.de

More available books at **www.hansebooks.com**

HOME BALLADS

AND

POEMS.

BY

JOHN GREENLEAF WHITTIER.

BOSTON:
TICKNOR AND FIELDS.
M DCCC LXI.

I CALL the old time back: I bring these lays
To thee, in memory of the summer days
When, by our native streams and forest ways,

We dreamed them over; while the rivulets made
Songs of their own, and the great pine-trees laid
On warm noon-lights the masses of their shade.

And she was with us, living o'er again
Her life in ours, despite of years and pain, —
The Autumn's brightness after latter rain.

Beautiful in her holy peace as one
Who stands, at evening, when the work is done,
Glorified in the setting of the sun!

Her memory makes our common landscape seem
Fairer than any of which painters dream,
Lights the brown hills and sings in every stream;

For she whose speech was always truth's pure gold
Heard, not unpleased, its simple legends told,
And loved with us the beautiful and old.

CONTENTS.

	PAGE
THE OVER-HEART,	101
IN REMEMBRANCE OF JOSEPH STURGE,	105
TRINITAS,	111
THE OLD BURYING-GROUND,	115
THE PIPES AT LUCKNOW,	120
MY PSALM,	125
LE MARAIS DU CYGNE,	129
"THE ROCK" IN EL GHOR,	133
ON A PRAYER-BOOK,	136
TO J. T. F.,	140
THE PALM-TREE,	144
LINES FOR THE BURNS FESTIVAL,	147
THE RED RIVER VOYAGEUR,	150
KENOZA LAKE,	153
TO G. B. C.,	156
THE SISTERS,	158
LINES FOR AN AGRICULTURAL EXHIBITION,	160
THE PREACHER,	162
THE QUAKER ALUMNI,	182
BROWN OF OSSAWATOMIE,	195
FROM PERUGIA,	198
FOR AN AUTUMN FESTIVAL,	204

BALLADS.

THE WITCH'S DAUGHTER.

It was the pleasant harvest time,
    When cellar-bins are closely stowed,
    And garrets bend beneath their load,

And the old swallow-haunted barns —
    Brown-gabled, long, and full of seams
    Through which the moted sunlight streams,

And winds blow freshly in, to shake
    The red plumes of the roosted cocks,
    And the loose hay-mow's scented locks —

Are filled with summer's ripened stores,
    Its odorous grass and barley sheaves,
    From their low scaffolds to their eaves.

On Esek Harden's oaken floor,
    With many an autumn threshing worn,
    Lay the heaped ears of unhusked corn.

And thither came young men and maids,
    Beneath a moon that, large and low,
    Lit that sweet eve of long ago.

They took their places; some by chance,
    And others by a merry voice
    Or sweet smile guided to their choice.

How pleasantly the rising moon,
    Between the shadow of the mows,
    Looked on them through the great elm boughs!—

On sturdy boyhood sun-embrowned,
    On girlhood with its solid curves
    Of healthful strength and painless nerves!

And jests went round, and laughs that made
    The house-dog answer with his howl,
    And kept astir the barn-yard fowl;

And quaint old songs their fathers sung,
    In Derby dales and Yorkshire moors,
    Ere Norman William trod their shores;

And tales, whose merry license shook
    The fat sides of the Saxon thane,
    Forgetful of the hovering Dane!

But still the sweetest voice was mute
    That river-valley ever heard,
    From lip of maid or throat of bird;

For Mabel Martin sat apart,
    And let the hay-mow's shadow fall
    Upon the loveliest face of all.

She sat apart, as one forbid,
    Who knew that none would condescend
    To own the Witch-wife's child a friend.

The seasons scarce had gone their round,
    Since curious thousands thronged to see
    Her mother on the gallows-tree;

And mocked the palsied limbs of age,
    That faltered on the fatal stairs,
    And wan lip trembling with its prayers!

Few questioned of the sorrowing child,
    Or, when they saw the mother die,
    Dreamed of the daughter's agony.

They went up to their homes that day,
    As men and Christians justified:
    God willed it, and the wretch had died!

Dear God and Father of us all,
    Forgive our faith in cruel lies, —
    Forgive the blindness that denies!

Forgive thy creature when he takes,
    For the all-perfect love thou art,
    Some grim creation of his heart.

Cast down our idols, overturn
    Our bloody altars; let us see
    Thyself in thy humanity!

Poor Mabel from her mother's grave
    Crept to her desolate hearth-stone,
    And wrestled with her fate alone;

With love, and anger, and despair,
  The phantoms of disordered sense,
  The awful doubts of Providence!

The school boys jeered her as they passed,
  And, when she sought the house of prayer,
  Her mother's curse pursued her there

And still o'er many a neighboring door
  She saw the horseshoe's curvéd charm,
  To guard against her mother's harm: —

That mother, poor, and sick, and lame,
  Who daily, by the old arm-chair,
  Folded her withered hands in prayer: —

Who turned, in Salem's dreary jail,
  Her worn old Bible o'er and o'er,
  When her dim eyes could read no more!

Sore tried and pained, the poor girl kept
  Her faith, and trusted that her way,
  So dark, would somewhere meet the day.

And still her weary wheel went round
    Day after day, with no relief;
    Small leisure have the poor for grief.

So in the shadow Mabel sits;
    Untouched by mirth she sees and hears,
    Her smile is sadder than her tears.

But cruel eyes have found her out,
    And cruel lips repeat her name,
    And taunt her with her mother's shame.

She answered not with railing words,
    But drew her apron o'er her face,
    And, sobbing, glided from the place.

And only pausing at the door,
    Her sad eyes met the troubled gaze
    Of one who, in her better days,

Had been her warm and steady friend,
    Ere yet her mother's doom had made
    Even Esek Harden half afraid.

He felt that mute appeal of tears,
　　And, starting, with an angry frown
　　Hushed all the wicked murmurs down.

"Good neighbors mine," he sternly said,
　　"This passes harmless mirth or jest;
　　I brook no insult to my guest.

"She is indeed her mother's child;
　　But God's sweet pity ministers
　　Unto no whiter soul than hers.

"Let Goody Martin rest in peace;
　　I never knew her harm a fly,
　　And witch or not, God knows — not I.

"I know who swore her life away;
　　And, as God lives, I 'd not condemn
　　An Indian dog on word of them."

The broadest lands in all the town,
　　The skill to guide, the power to awe,
　　Were Harden's; and his word was law.

None dared withstand him to his face,
  But one sly maiden spake aside:
  "The little witch is evil eyed!

"Her mother only killed a cow,
  Or witched a churn or dairy-pan;
  But she, forsooth, must charm a man!"

Poor Mabel, in her lonely home,
  Sat by the window's narrow pane,
  White in the moonlight's silver rain.

The river, on its pebbled rim,
  Made music such as childhood knew;
  The door-yard tree was whispered through

By voices such as chilhood's ear
  Had heard in moonlights long ago;
  And through the willow boughs below

She saw the rippled water shine;
  Beyond, in waves of shade and light,
  The hills rolled off into the night.

Sweet sounds and pictures mocking so
    The sadness of her human lot,
    She saw and heard, but heeded not.

She strove to drown her sense of wrong,
    And, in her old and simple way,
    To teach her bitter heart to pray.

Poor child! the prayer, begun in faith,
    Grew to a low, despairing cry
    Of utter misery: " Let me die!

" Oh! take me from the scornful eyes,
    And hide me where the cruel speech
    And mocking finger may not reach!

" I dare not breathe my mother's name:
    A daughter's right I dare not crave
    To weep above her unblest grave!

"Let me not live until my heart,
    With few to pity, and with none
    To love me, hardens into stone.

"Oh God! have mercy on thy child,
  Whose faith in thee grows weak and small,
  And take me ere I lose it all!"

A shadow on the moonlight fell,
  And murmuring wind and wave became
  A voice whose burden was her name.

Had then God heard her? Had he sent
  His angel down? In flesh and blood,
  Before her Esek Harden stood!

He laid his hand upon her arm:
  "Dear Mabel, this no more shall be;
  Who scoffs at you, must scoff at me.

"You know rough Esek Harden well;
  And if he seems no suitor gay,
  And if his hair is touched with gray,

"The maiden grown shall never find
  His heart less warm than when she smiled,
  Upon his knees, a little child!"

Her tears of grief were tears of joy,
    As, folded in his strong embrace,
    She looked in Esek Harden's face.

"Oh, truest friend of all!" she said,
    "God bless you for your kindly thought,
    And make me worthy of my lot!"

He led her through his dewy fields,
    To where the swinging lanterns glowed,
    And through the doors the huskers showed.

"Good friends and neighbors!" Esek said,
    "I'm weary of this lonely life;
    In Mabel see my chosen wife!

"She greets you kindly, one and all;
    The past is past, and all offence
    Falls harmless from her innocence.

"Henceforth she stands no more alone;
    You know what Esek Harden is; —
    He brooks no wrong to him or his."

Now let the merriest tales be told,
    And let the sweetest songs be sung,
    That ever made the old heart young!

For now the lost has found a home;
    And a lone hearth shall brighter burn,
    As all the household joys return!

Oh, pleasantly the harvest moon,
    Between the shadow of the mows,
    Looked on them through the great elm boughs!

On Mabel's curls of golden hair,
    On Esek's shaggy strength it fell;
    And the wind whispered, "It is well!"

THE GARRISON OF CAPE ANN.

From the hills of home forth looking, far beneath the tent-like span
Of the sky, I see the white gleam of the headland of Cape Ann.
Well I know its coves and beaches to the ebb-tide glimmering down,
And the white-walled hamlet children of its ancient fishing town.

Long has passed the summer morning, and its memory waxes old,
When along yon breezy headlands with a pleasant friend I strolled.
Ah! the autumn sun is shining, and the ocean wind blows cool,
And the golden-rod and aster bloom around thy grave, Rantoul!

With the memory of that morning by the summer
    sea I blend
A wild and wondrous story, by the younger Mather
    penned,
In that quaint *Magnalia Christi*, with all strange and
    marvellous things,
Heaped up huge and undigested, like the chaos Ovid
    sings.

Dear to me these far, faint glimpses of the dual life
    of old,
Inward, grand with awe and reverence; outward,
    mean and coarse and cold;
Gleams of mystic beauty playing over dull and vul-
    gar clay,
Golden threads of romance weaving in a web of hod-
    den gray.

The great eventful Present hides the Past; but
    through the din
Of its loud life, hints and echoes from the life behind
    steal in;

And the lore of home and fireside, and the legendary
    rhyme,
Make the task of duty lighter which the true man
    owes his time.

So, with something of the feeling which the Cove-
    nanter knew,
When with pious chisel wandering Scotland's moor-
    land graveyards through,
From the graves of old traditions I part the black-
    berry vines,
Wipe the moss from off the head-stones, and retouch
    the faded lines.

Where the sea-waves back and forward, hoarse with
    rolling pebbles, ran,
The garrison-house stood watching on the gray
    rocks of Cape Ann;
On its windy site uplifting gabled roof and pali-
    sade
And rough walls of unhewn timber with the moon-
    light overlaid.

On his slow round walked the sentry, south and eastward looking forth
O'er a rude and broken coast-line, white with breakers stretching north, —
Wood and rock and gleaming sand-drift, jagged capes, with bush and tree,
Leaning inland from the smiting of the wild and gusty sea.

Before the deep-mouthed chimney, dimly lit by dying brands,
Twenty soldiers sat and waited, with their muskets in their hands;
On the rough-hewn oaken table the venison haunch was shared,
And the pewter tankard circled slowly round from beard to beard.

Long they sat and talked together, — talked of wizards Satan-sold;
Of all ghostly sights and noises, — signs and wonders manifold;

Of the spectre-ship of Salem, with the dead men in
    her shrouds,
Sailing sheer above the water, in the loom of morn-
    ing clouds;

Of the marvellous valley hidden in the depth of
    Gloucester woods,
Full of plants that love the summer — blooms of
    warmer latitudes;
Where the Arctic birch is braided by the tropic's
    flowery vines,
And the white magnolia blossoms star the twilight
    of the pines!

But their voices sank yet lower, sank to husky tones
    of fear,
As they spake of present tokens of the powers of
    evil near;
Of a spectral host, defying stroke of steel and aim
    of gun;
Never yet was ball to slay them in the mould of
    mortals run!

Thrice, with plumes and flowing scalp-locks, from the midnight wood they came, —
Thrice around the block-house marching, met, unharmed, its volleyed flame;
Then, with mocking laugh and gesture, sunk in earth or lost in air,
All the ghostly wonder vanished, and the moon-lit sands lay bare.

Midnight came; from out the forest moved a dusky mass, that soon
Grew to warriors, plumed and painted, grimly marching in the moon.
"Ghosts or witches," said the captain, "thus I foil the Evil One!"
And he rammed a silver button, from his doublet, down his gun.

Once again the spectral horror moved the guarded wall about;
Once again the levelled muskets through the palisades flashed out,

With that deadly aim the squirrel on his tree-top
    might not shun,
Nor the beach-bird seaward flying with his slant
    wing to the sun.

Like the idle rain of summer sped the harmless
    shower of lead.
With a laugh of fierce derision, once again the phan-
    toms fled;
Once again, without a shadow on the sands the
    moonlight lay,
And the white smoke curling through it drifted
    slowly down the bay!

"God preserve us!" said the captain; "never mor-
    tal foes were there:
They have vanished with their leader, Prince and
    Power of the Air!
Lay aside your useless weapons: skill and prowess
    naught avail;
They who do the devil's service, wear their master's
    coat of mail!"

So the night grew near to cock-crow, when again a
    warning call
Roused the score of weary soldiers watching round
    the dusky hall;
And they looked to flint and priming, and they
    longed for break of day;
But the captain closed his Bible: "Let us cease
    from man, and pray!"

To the men who went before us, all the unseen
    powers seemed near,
And their steadfast strength of courage struck its
    roots in holy fear.
Every hand forsook the musket, every head was
    bowed and bare,
Every stout knee pressed the flag-stones, as the cap-
    tain led in prayer.

Ceased thereat the mystic marching of the spectres
    round the wall,
But a sound abhorred, unearthly, smote the ears
    and hearts of all,—

Howls of rage and shrieks of anguish! Never after mortal man
Saw the ghostly leaguers marching round the blockhouse of Cape Ann.

So to us who walk in summer through the cool and sea-blown town,
From the childhood of its people comes the solemn legend down.
Not in vain the ancient fiction, in whose moral lives the youth
And the fitness and the freshness of an undecaying truth.

Soon or late to all our dwellings come the spectres of the mind,
Doubts and fears and dread forebodings, in the darkness undefined;
Round us throng the grim projections of the heart and of the brain,
And our pride of strength is weakness, and the cunning hand is vain.

In the dark we cry like children; and no answer from on high
Breaks the crystal spheres of silence, and no white wings downward fly;
But the heavenly help we pray for comes to faith, and not to sight,
And our prayers themselves drive backward all the spirits of the night!

THE PROPHECY OF SAMUEL SEWALL.

1697.

Up and down the village streets
Strange are the forms my fancy meets,
For the thoughts and things of to-day are hid,
And through the vail of a closed lid
The ancient worthies I see again:
I hear the tap of the elder's cane,
And his awful periwig I see,
And the silver buckles of shoe and knee.
Stately and slow, with thoughtful air,
His black cap hiding his whitened hair,
Walks the Judge of the Great Assize,
Samuel Sewall the good and wise.
His face with lines of firmness wrought,
He wears the look of a man unbought
Who swears to his hurt and changes not;

Yet, touched and softened nevertheless
With the grace of Christian gentleness,
The face that a child would climb to kiss!
True, and tender, and brave, and just,
That man might honor and woman trust!

Touching and sad, a tale is told,
Like a penitent hymn of the Psalmist old,
Of the fast which the good man life-long kept
With a haunting sorrow that never slept,
As the circling year brought round the time
Of an error that left the sting of crime,
When he sat on the bench of the witchcraft courts,
With the laws of Moses and Hale's Reports,
And spake, in the name of both, the word
That gave the witch's neck to the cord,
And piled the oaken planks that pressed
The feeble life from the warlock's breast!
All the day long, from dawn to dawn,
His door was bolted, his curtain drawn;
No foot on his silent threshold trod,
No eye looked on him save that of God,

As he baffled the ghosts of the dead with charms
Of penitent tears, and prayers, and psalms,
And, with precious proofs from the sacred word
Of the boundless pity and love of the Lord,
His faith confirmed and his trust renewed
That the sin of his ignorance sorely rued,
Might be washed away in the mingled flood
Of his human sorrow and Christ's dear blood!

  Green forever the memory be
Of the Judge of the old Theocracy,
Whom even his errors glorified,
Like a far-seen, sunlit mountain-side
By the cloudy shadows which o'er it glide!
Honor and praise to the Puritan
Who the halting step of his age outran,
And, seeing the infinite worth of man
In the priceless gift the Father gave,
In the infinite love that stooped to save,
Dared not brand his brother a slave!
"Who doth such wrong," he was wont to say,
In his own quaint, picture-loving way,

"Flings up to Heaven a hand grenade
Which God shall cast down upon his head!"

Widely as heaven and hell, contrast
That brave old jurist of the past
And the cunning trickster and knave of courts
Who the holy features of Truth distorts, —
Ruling as right the will of the strong,
Poverty, crime, and weakness wrong;
Wide-eared to power, to the wronged and weak
Deaf as Egypt's gods of leek;
Scoffing aside at party's nod
Order of nature and law of God;
For whose dabbled ermine respect were waste,
Reverence folly, and awe misplaced;
Justice of whom 'twere vain to seek
As from Koordish robber or Syrian Sheik!
Oh! leave the wretch to his bribes and sins,
Let him rot in the web of lies he spins!
To the saintly soul of the early day, —
To the Christian judge, let us turn and say:
"Praise and thanks, for an honest man! —
Glory to God for the Puritan!"

I see, far southward, this quiet day,
The hills of Newbury rolling away,
With the many tints of the season gay,
Dreamily blending in autumn mist
Crimson, and gold, and amethyst.
Long and low, with dwarf trees crowned,
Plum Island lies, like a whale aground,
A stone's toss over the narrow sound.
Inland, as far as the eye can go,
The hills curve round like a bended bow;
A silver arrow from out them sprung,
I see the shine of the Quasycung;
And, round and round, over valley and hill,
Old roads winding, as old roads will,
Here to a ferry, and there to a mill:
And glimpses of chimneys and gabled eaves,
Through green elm arches and maple leaves, —
Old homsteads sacred to all that can
Gladden or sadden the heart of man, —
Over whose thresholds of oak and stone
Life and Death have come and gone!
There pictured tiles in the fire-place show,
Great beams sag from the ceiling low,

The dresser glitters with polished wares,
The long clock ticks on the foot-worn stairs;
And the low, broad chimney shows the crack
By the earthquake made a century back.
Up from their midst springs the village spire
With the crest of its cock in the sun afire;
Beyond are orchards and planting lands,
And great salt marshes and glimmering sands,
And, where north and south the coast-lines run,
The blink of the sea in breeze and sun!

I see it all like a chart unrolled,
But my thoughts are full of the past and old,
I hear the tales of my boyhood told;
And the shadows and shapes of early days
Flit dimly by in the vailing haze,
With measured movement and rhythmic chime
Weaving like shuttles, my web of rhyme.
I think of the old man wise and good
Who once on yon misty hillsides stood
(A poet who never measured rhyme,
A seer unknown to his dull-eared time),

And, propped on his staff of age, looked down,
With his boyhood's love, on his native town,
Where, written, as if on its hills and plains,
His burden of prophecy yet remains,
For the voices of wood, and wave, and wind
To read in the ear of the musing mind: —

"As long as Plum Island, to guard the coast
As God appointed, shall keep its post;
As long as a salmon shall haunt the deep
Of Merrimac river, or sturgeon leap;
As long as pickerel swift and slim,
Or red-backed perch, in Crane Pond swim;
As long as the annual sea-fowl know
Their time to come and their time to go.
As long as cattle shall roam at will
The green, grass meadows by Turkey Hill;
As long as sheep shall look from the side
Of Oldtown Hill on marishes wide,
And Parker River, and salt-sea tide.
As long as a wandering pigeon shall search
The fields below from his white-oak perch,

When the barley-harvest is ripe and shorn
And the dry husks fall from the standing corn;
As long as Nature shall not grow old,
Nor drop her work from her doting hold,
And her care for the Indian corn forget,
And the yellow rows in pairs to set;—
So long shall Christians here be born,
Grow up and ripen as God's sweet corn!—
By the beak of bird, by the breath of frost
Shall never a holy ear be lost,
But, husked by Death in the Planter's sight,
Be sown again in the fields of light!"

The Island still is purple with plums,
Up the river the salmon comes,
The sturgeon leaps, and the wild fowl feeds
On hill-side berries and marish seeds,—
All the beautiful signs remain,
From spring-time sowing to autumn rain
The good man's vision returns again!
And let us hope, as well we can,
That the Silent Angel who garners man

May find some grain as of old he found
In the human corn-field ripe and sound,
And the Lord of the Harvest deign to own
The precious seed by the fathers sown!

SKIPPER IRESON'S RIDE.

Of all the rides since the birth of time,
Told in story or sung in rhyme, —
On Apuleius's Golden Ass,
Or one-eyed Calendar's horse of brass,
Witch astride of a human hack,
Islam's prophet on Al-Borák, —
The strangest ride that ever was sped
Was Ireson's, out from Marblehead!
  Old Floyd Ireson, for his hard heart,
   Tarred and feathered and carried in a cart
  By the women of Marblehead!

Body of turkey, head of owl,
Wings a-droop like a rained-on fowl,
Feathered and ruffled in every part,
Skipper Ireson stood in the cart.
Scores of women, old and young,
Strong of muscle, and glib of tongue,

Pushed and pulled up the rocky lane,
Shouting and singing the shrill refrain :
    "Here's Flud Oirson, fur his horrd horrt,
    Torr'd an' futherr'd an' corr'd in a corrt
    By the women o' Morble'ead!"

Wrinkled scolds with hands on hips,
Girls in bloom of cheek and lips,
Wild-eyed, free-limbed, such as chase
Bacchus round some antique vase,
Brief of skirt, with ankles bare,
Loose of kerchief and loose of hair,
With conch-shells blowing and fish-horns' twang,
Over and over the Mænads sang :
    "Here's Flud Oirson, fur his horrd horrt,
    Torr'd an' futherr'd an' corr'd in a corrt
    By the women o' Morble'ead!"

Small pity for him! — He sailed away
From a leaking ship, in Chaleur Bay, —
Sailed away from a sinking wreck,
With his own town's-people on her deck!

"Lay by! lay by!" they called to him.
Back he answered, "Sink or swim!
Brag of your catch of fish again!"
And off he sailed through the fog and rain!
    Old Floyd Ireson, for his hard heart,
      Tarred and feathered and carried in a cart
        By the women of Marblehead!

Fathoms deep in dark Chaleur
That wreck shall lie forevermore.
Mother and sister, wife and maid,
Looked from the rocks of Marblehead
Over the moaning and rainy sea, —
Looked for the coming that might not be!
What did the winds and the sea-birds say
Of the cruel captain who sailed away? —
    Old Floyd Ireson, for his hard heart,
      Tarred and feathered and carried in a cart
        By the women of Marblehead!

Through the street, on either side,
Up flew windows, doors swung wide;

Sharp-tongued spinsters, old wives gray,
Treble lent the fish-horn's bray.
Sea-worn grandsires, cripple-bound,
Hulks of old sailors run aground,
Shook head, and fist, and hat, and cane,
And cracked with curses the hoarse refrain:
    "Here's Flud Oirson, fur his horrd horrt,
    Torr'd an' futherr'd an' corr'd in a corrt
      By the women o' Morble'ead!"

Sweetly along the Salem road
Bloom of orchard and lilac showed.
Little the wicked skipper knew
Of the fields so green and the sky so blue.
Riding there in his sorry trim,
Like an Indian idol glum and grim,
Scarcely he seemed the sound to hear
Of voices shouting far and near:
    "Here's Flud Oirson, fur his horrd horrt,
    Torr'd an' futherr'd an' corr'd in a corrt
      By the women o' Morble'ead!"

"Hear me, neighbors!" at last he cried, —
"What to me is this noisy ride?
What is the shame that clothes the skin
To the nameless horror that lives within?
Waking or sleeping, I see a wreck,
And hear a cry from a reeling deck!
Hate me and curse me, — I only dread
The hand of God and the face of the dead!"
    Said old Floyd Ireson, for his hard heart,
    Tarred and feathered and carried in a cart
    By the women of Marblehead!

Then the wife of the skipper lost at sea
Said, "God has touched him! — why should we?"
Said an old wife mourning her only son,
"Cut the rogue's tether and let him run!"
So with soft relentings and rude excuse,
Half scorn, half pity, they cut him loose,
And gave him a cloak to hide him in,
And left him alone with his shame and sin.
    Poor Floyd Ireson, for his hard heart,
    Tarred and feathered and carried in a cart
    By the women of Marblehead!

TELLING THE BEES.*

Here is the place; right over the hill
   Runs the path I took;
You can see the gap in the old wall still,
   And the stepping-stones in the shallow brook.

There is the house, with the gate red-barred,
   And the poplars tall;
And the barn's brown length, and the cattle-yard,
   And the white horns tossing above the wall

There are the bee-hives ranged in the sun;
   And down by the brink
Of the brook are her poor flowers, weed-o'errun,
   Pansy and daffodil, rose and pink.

---

* A remarkable custom, brought from the Old Country, formerly prevailed in the rural districts of New England. On the death of a member of the family, the bees were at once informed of the event, and their hives dressed in mourning. This ceremonial was supposed to be necessary to prevent the swarms from leaving their hives and seeking a new home.

A year has gone, as the tortoise goes,
    Heavy and slow;
And the same rose blows, and the same sun glows,
    And the same brook sings of a year ago.

There's the same sweet clover-smell in the breeze;
    And the June sun warm
Tangles his wings of fire in the trees,
    Setting, as then, over Fernside farm.

I mind me how with a lover's care
    From my Sunday coat
I brushed off the burs, and smoothed my hair,
    And cooled at the brook-side my brow and throat.

Since we parted, a month had passed, —
    To love, a year;
Down through the beeches I looked at last
    On the little red gate and the well-sweep near.

I can see it all now, — the slantwise rain
    Of light through the leaves,
The sundown's blaze on her window-pane,
    The bloom of her roses under the eaves.

Just the same as a month before, —
    The house and the trees,
The barn's brown gable, the vine by the door, —
    Nothing changed but the hives of bees.

Before them, under the garden wall,
    Forward and back,
Went drearily singing the chore-girl small,
    Draping each hive with a shred of black

Trembling, I listened: the summer sun
    Had the chill of snow;
For I knew she was telling the bees of one
    Gone on the journey we all must go!

Then I said to myself, "My Mary weeps
    For the dead to-day:
Haply her blind old grandsire sleeps
    The fret and the pain of his age away."

But her dog whined low; on the doorway sill,
    With his cane to his chin,
The old man sat; and the chore-girl still
    Sung to the bees stealing out and in.

And the song she was singing ever since
In my ear sounds on : —
"Stay at home, pretty bees, fly not hence!
Mistress Mary is dead and gone!"

THE SYCAMORES.

In the outskirts of the village,
   On the river's winding shores,
Stand the Occidental plane-trees,
   Stand the ancient sycamores.

One long century hath been numbered,
   And another half-way told,
Since the rustic Irish gleeman
   Broke for them the virgin mould.

Deftly set to Celtic music,
   At his violin's sound they grew,
Through the moonlit eves of summer,
   Making Amphion's fable true.

Rise again, thou poor Hugh Tallant!
   Pass in jerkin green along,
With thy eyes brim full of laughter,
   And thy mouth as full of song.

Pioneer of Erin's outcasts,
  With his fiddle and his pack;
Little dreamed the village Saxons
  Of the myriads at his back.

How he wrought with spade and fiddle,
  Delved by day and sang by night,
With a hand that never wearied,
  And a heart forever light, —

Still the gay tradition mingles
  With a record grave and drear,
Like the rolic air of Cluny,
  With the solemn march of Mear.

When the box-tree, white with blossoms,
  Made the sweet May woodlands glad.
And the Aronia by the river
  Lighted up the swarming shad,

And the bulging nets swept shoreward,
  With their silver-sided haul,
Midst the shouts of dripping fishers,
  He was merriest of them all.

When, among the jovial huskers,
    Love stole in at Labor's side,
With the lusty airs of England,
    Soft his Celtic measures vied.

Songs of love and wailing lyke-wake,
    And the merry fair's carouse;
Of the wild Red Fox of Erin
    And the Woman of Three Cows,

By the blazing hearths of Winter,
    Pleasant seemed his simple tales,
Midst the grimmer Yorkshire legends,
    And the mountain myths of Wales.

How the souls in Purgatory
    Scrambled up from fate forlorn,
On St. Keven's sackcloth ladder,
    Slyly hitched to Satan's horn.

Of the fiddler who at Tara
    Played all night to ghosts of kings;
Of the brown dwarfs, and the fairies
    Dancing in their moorland rings!

Jolliest of our birds of singing,
    Best he loved the Bob-o-link.
"Hush!" he 'd say, "the tipsy fairies♭
    Hear the little folks in drink!"

Merry-faced, with spade and fiddle,
    Singing through the ancient town,
Only this, of poor Hugh Tallant,
    Hath Tradition handed down.

Not a stone his grave discloses;
    But if yet his spirit walks,
'T is beneath the trees he planted,
    And when Bob-o-Lincoln talks!

Green memorials of the gleeman!
    Linking still the river shores,
With their shadows cast by sunset,
    Stand Hugh Tallant's sycamores!

When the Father of his Country
    Through the north-land riding came,
And the roofs were starred with banners,
    And the steeples rang acclaim, —

When each war-scarred Continental,
    Leaving smithy, mill, and farm,
Waved his rusted sword in welcome,
    And shot off his old king's-arm, —

Slowly passed that august Presence
    Down the thronged and shouting street;
Village girls, as white as angels,
    Scattering flowers around his feet.

Midway, where the plane-tree's shadow
    Deepest fell, his rein he drew:
On his stately head, uncovered,
    Cool and soft the west wind blew.

And he stood up in his stirrups,
    Looking up and looking down
On the hills of Gold and Silver
    Rimming round the little town, —

On the river, full of sunshine,
    To the lap of greenest vales,
Winding down from wooded headlands,
    Willow-skirted, white with sails

And he said, the landscape sweeping
    Slowly with his ungloved hand,
" I have seen no prospect fairer
    In this goodly Eastern land."

Then the bugles of his escort
    Stirred to life the cavalcade:
And that head, so bare and stately,
    Vanished down the depths of shade.

Ever since, in town and farm-house,
    Life has had its ebb and flow;
Thrice hath passed the human harvest
    To its garner green and low.

But the trees the gleeman planted,
    Through the changes, changeless stand;
As the marble calm of Tadmor
    Marks the desert's shifting sand.

Still the level moon at rising
    Silvers o'er each stately shaft;
Still beneath them, half in shadow,
    Singing, glides the pleasure craft.

Still beneath them, arm-enfolded,
    Love and Youth together stray ;
While, as heart to heart beats faster,
    More and more their feet delay.

Where the ancient cobbler, Keezar,
    On the open hill-side wrought,
Singing, as he drew his stitches,
    Songs his German masters taught.

Singing, with his gray hair floating
    Round his rosy ample face ;
Now a thousand Saxon craftsmen
    Stitch and hammer in his place.

All the pastoral lanes so grassy,
    Now are Traffic's dusty streets ;
From the village, grown a city,
    Fast the rural grace retreats.

But, still green, and tall, and stately,
    On the river's winding shores,
Stand the Occidental plane-trees,
    Stand Hugh Tallant's sycamores

THE DOUBLE-HEADED SNAKE OF NEWBURY.

"Concerning yͤ Amphisbæna, as soon as I received your commands, I made diligent inquiry : . . . . . he assures me yᵗ it had really two heads, one at each end ; two mouths, two stings or tongues."

REV. CHRISTOPHER TOPPAN *to* COTTON MATHER.

FAR away in the twilight time
Of every people, in every clime,
Dragons and griffins and monsters dire,
Born of water, and air, and fire,
Or nursed, like the Python, in the mud
And ooze of the old Deucalion flood,
Crawl and wriggle and foam with rage,
Through dusk tradition and ballad age.
So from the childhood of Newbury town
And its time of fable the tale comes down
Of a terror which haunted bush and brake,
The Amphisbæna, the Double Snake !

Thou who makest the tale thy mirth,
Consider that strip of Christian earth
On the desolate shore of a sailless sea,
Full of terror and mystery,
Half-redeemed from the evil hold
Of the wood so dreary, and dark, and old,
Which drank with its lips of leaves the dew
When Time was young, and the world was new,
And wove its shadows with sun and moon,
Ere the stones of Cheops were squared and hewn;
Think of the sea's dread monotone,
Of the mournful wail from the pine-wood blown,
Of the strange, vast splendors that lit the North,
Of the troubled throes of the quaking earth,
And the dismal tales the Indian told,
Till the settler's heart at his hearth grew cold,
And he shrank from the tawny wizard's boasts,
And the hovering shadows seemed full of ghosts,
And above, below, and on every side,
The fear of his creed seemed verified; —
And think, if his lot were now thine own,
To grope with terrors nor named nor known,

How laxer muscle and weaker nerve
And a feebler faith thy need might serve;
And own to thyself the wonder more
That the snake had two heads, and not a score!

Whether he lurked in the Oldtown fen,
Or the gray earth-flax of the Devil's Den,
Or swam in the wooded Artichoke,
Or coiled by the Northman's Written Rock,
Nothing on record is left to show;
Only the fact that he lived, we know,
And left the cast of a double head
In the scaly mask which he yearly shed.
For he carried a head where his tail should be,
And the two, of course, could never agree,
But wriggled about with main and might,
Now to the left and now to the right;
Pulling and twisting this way and that,
Neither knew what the other was at.

A snake with two heads, lurking so near!—
Judge of the wonder, guess at the fear!

Think what ancient gossips might say,
Shaking their heads in their dreary way,
Between the meetings on Sabbath-day!
How urchins, searching at day's decline
The Common Pasture for sheep or kine,
The terrible double-ganger heard
In leafy rustle or whirr of bird!
Think what a zest it gave to the sport,
In berry-time of the younger sort,
As over pastures blackberry-twined
Reuben and Dorothy lagged behind,
And closer and closer, for fear of harm,
The maiden clung to her lover's arm;
And how the spark, who was forced to stay,
By his sweetheart's fears, till the break of day,
Thanked the snake for the fond delay!

Far and wide the tale was told,
Like a snowball growing while it rolled.
The nurse hushed with it the baby's cry;
And it served, in the worthy minister's eye,
To paint the primitive serpent by.

Cotton Mather came galloping down
All the way to Newbury town,
With his eyes agog and his ears set wide,
And his marvellous inkhorn at his side;
Stirring the while in the shallow pool
Of his brains for the lore he learned at school,
To garnish the story, with here a streak
Of Latin, and there another of Greek:
And the tales he heard and the notes he took,
Behold! are they not in his Wonder-Book?

Stories, like dragons, are hard to kill.
If the snake does not, the tale runs still
In Byfield Meadows, on Pipestave Hill.
And still, whenever husband and wife
Publish the shame of their daily strife,
And, with mad cross-purpose, tug and strain
At either end of the marriage-chain,
The gossips say, with a knowing shake
Of their gray heads, "Look at the Double Snake!
One in body and two in will,
The Amphisbæna is living still!"

THE SWAN SONG OF PARSON AVERY.

WHEN the reaper's task was ended, and the summer wearing late,
Parson Avery sailed from Newbury, with his wife and children eight,
Dropping down the river-harbor in the shallop "Watch and Wait."

Pleasantly lay the clearings in the mellow summer-morn,
With the newly-planted orchards dropping their fruits first-born,
And the homesteads like green islands amid a sea of corn.

Broad meadows reached out seaward the tided
    creeks between,
And hills rolled wave-like inland, with oaks and wal-
    nuts green; —
A fairer home, a goodlier land his eyes had never
    seen.

Yet away sailed Parson Avery, away where duty
    led,
And the voice of God seemed calling, to break the
    living bread
To the souls of fishers starving on the rocks of
    Marblehead.

All day they sailed: at nightfall the pleasant land-
    breeze died,
The blackening sky, at midnight, its starry lights
    denied,
And far and low the thunder of tempest prophe-
    sied!

Blotted out were all the coast-lines, gone were rock,
    and wood, and sand;
Grimly anxious stood the skipper with the rudder in
    his hand,
And questioned of the darkness what was sea and
    what was land.

And the preacher heard his dear ones, nestled round
    him, weeping sore:
"Never heed, my little children! Christ is walking
    on before
To the pleasant land of heaven, where the sea shall
    be no more."

All at once the great cloud parted, like a curtain
    drawn aside,
To let down the torch of lightning on the terror far
    and wide;
And the thunder and the whirlwind together smote
    the tide.

There was wailing in the shallop, woman's wail and
    man's despair,
A crash of breaking timbers on the rocks so sharp
    and bare,
And, through it all, the murmur of Father Avery's
    prayer.

From his struggle in the darkness with the wild
    waves and the blast,
On a rock, where every billow broke above him as
    it passed,
Alone, of all his household, the man of God was
    cast.

There a comrade heard him praying, in the pause of
    wave and wind:
"All my own have gone before me, and I linger just
    behind;
Not for life I ask, but only for the rest thy ransomed
    find!

"In this night of death I challenge the promise of
   thy word! —
Let me see the great salvation of which mine ears
   have heard! —
Let me pass from hence forgiven, through the grace
   of Christ, our Lord!

In the baptism of these waters wash white my every
   sin,
And let me follow up to thee my household and my
   kin!
Open the sea-gate of thy heaven, and let me enter
   in!"

When the christian sings his death-song, all the
   listening heavens draw near,
And the angels, leaning over the walls of crystal,
   hear
How the notes so faint and broken swell to music in
   God's ear.

The ear of God was open to his servant's last request;
As the strong wave swept him downward the sweet hymn upward pressed,
And the soul of Father Avery went, singing, to its rest.

There was wailing on the mainland, from the rocks of Marblehead;
In the stricken church of Newbury the notes of prayer were read;
And long, by board and hearth-stone, the living mourned the dead.

And still the fishers outbound, or scudding from the squall,
With grave and reverent faces, the ancient tale recall,
When they see the white waves breaking on the Rock of Avery's Fall!

THE TRUCE OF PISCATAQUA.

1675.

Raze these long blocks of brick and stone,
These huge mill-monsters overgrown:
Blot out the humbler piles as well,
Where, moved like living shuttles, dwell
The weaving genii of the bell:
Tear from the wild Cocheco's track
The dams that hold its torrents back;
And let the loud-rejoicing fall
Plunge, roaring, down its rocky wall;
And let the Indian's paddle play
On the unbridged Piscataqua!
Wide over hill and valley spread
Once more the forest, dusk and dread,
With here and there a clearing cut
From the walled shadows round it shut;

Each with its farm-house builded rude,
By English yeoman squared and hewed,
And the grim, flankered block-house bound
With bristling palisades around.
So, haply, shall before thine eyes
The dusty vail of centuries rise,
The old, strange scenery overlay
The tamer pictures of to-day,
While, like the actors in a play,
Pass in their ancient guise along
The figures of my border song:
What time beside Cocheco's flood
The white man and the red man stood,
With words of peace and brotherhood;
When passed the sacred calumet
From lip to lip with fire-draught wet,
And, puffed in scorn, the peace-pipe's smoke
Through the gray beard of Waldron broke,
And Squando's voice, in suppliant plea
For mercy, struck the haughty key
Of one who held, in any fate,
His native pride inviolate!

THE TRUCE OF PISCATAQUA.

"Let your ears be opened wide!
He who speaks has never lied.
Waldron of Piscataqua,
Hear what Squando has to say!

"Squando shuts his eyes and sees,
Far off, Saco's hemlock-trees.
In his wigwam, still as stone,
Sits a woman all alone,

"Wampum beads and birchen strands
Dropping from her careless hands,
Listening ever for the fleet
Patter of a dead child's feet!

"When the moon a year ago
Told the flowers the time to blow,
In that lonely wigwam smiled
Menewee, our little child.

"Ere that moon grew thin and old,
He was lying still and cold;
Sent before us, weak and small,
When the Master did not call!

"On his little grave I lay;
Three times went and came the day;
Thrice above me blazed the noon,
Thrice upon me wept the moon.

"In the third night watch I heard,
Far and low, a spirit-bird;
Very mournful, very wild,
Sang the totem of my child.

"'Menewee, poor Menewee,
Walks a path he cannot see:
Let the white man's wigwam light
With its blaze his steps aright.

"'All-uncalled, he dares not show
Empty hands to Manito:
Better gifts he cannot bear
Than the scalps his slayers wear.'

"All the while the totem sang,
Lightning blazed and thunder rang;
And a black cloud, reaching high,
Pulled the white moon from the sky.

"I, the medicine-man, whose ear
All that spirits hear can hear, —
I, whose eyes are wide to see
All the things that are to be, —

"Well I knew the dreadful signs
In the whispers of the pines,
In the river roaring loud,
In the mutter of the cloud.

"At the breaking of the day,
From the grave I passed away;
Flowers bloomed round me, birds sang glad,
But my heart was hot and mad.

"There is rust on Squando's knife,
From the warm, red springs of life;
On the funeral hemlock-trees
Many a scalp the totem sees.

"Blood for blood! But evermore
Squando's heart is sad and sore;
And his poor squaw waits at home
For the feet that never come!

"Waldron of Cocheco, hear!
Squando speaks, who laughs at fear:
Take the captives he has ta'en;
Let the land have peace again!"

As the words died on his tongue,
Wide apart his warriors swung;
Parted, at the sign he gave,
Right and left, like Egypt's wave.

And, like Israel passing free
Through the prophet-charmed sea,
Captive mother, wife, and child
Through the dusky terror filed.

One alone, a little maid,
Middleway her steps delayed,
Glancing, with quick, troubled sight,
Round about from red to white.

Then his hand the Indian laid
On the little maiden's head,
Lightly from her forehead fair
Smoothing back her yellow hair.

"Gift or favor ask I none;
What I have is all my own:
Never yet the birds have sung,
'Squando hath a beggar's tongue.'

"Yet, for her who waits at home
For the dead who cannot come,
Let the little Gold-hair be
In the place of Menewee!

"Mishanock, my little star!
Come to Saco's pines afar:
Where the sad one waits at home,
Wequashim, my moonlight, come!"

"What!" quoth Waldron, "leave a child
Christian-born to heathens wild?
As God lives, from Satan's hand
I will pluck her as a brand!"

"Hear me, white man!" Squando cried;
"Let the little one decide.
Wequashim, my moonlight, say,
Wilt thou go with me, or stay?"

Slowly, sadly, half-afraid,
Half-regretfully, the maid
Owned the ties of blood and race, —
Turned from Squando's pleading face.

Not a word the Indian spoke,
But his wampum chain he broke,
And the beaded wonder hung
On that neck so fair and young.

Silence-shod, as phantoms seem
In the marches of a dream,
Single-filed, the grim array
Through the pine-trees wound away.

Doubting, trembling, sore amazed,
Through her tears the young child gazed.
"God preserve her!" Waldron said;
"Satan hath bewitched the maid!"

Years went and came. At close of day
Singing came a child from play,
Tossing from her loose-locked head
Gold in sunshine, brown in shade.

THE TRUCE OF PISCATAQUA.

Pride was in the mother's look,
But her head she gravely shook,
And with lips that fondly smiled
Feigned to chide her truant child.

Unabashed, the maid began:
"Up and down the brook I ran,
Where, beneath the bank so steep,
Lie the spotted trout asleep.

"'Chip!' went squirrel on the wall,
After me I heard him call,
And the cat-bird on the tree
Tried his best to mimic me.

"Where the hemlocks grew so dark
That I stopped to look and hark,
On a log, with feather-hat,
By the path, an Indian sat.

"Then I cried, and ran away;
But he called, and bade me stay;
And his voice was good and mild
As my mother's to her child.

"And he took my wampum chain,
Looked and looked it o'er again;
Gave me berries, and, beside,
On my neck a plaything tied."

Straight the mother stooped to see
What the Indian's gift might be.
On the braid of wampum hung,
Lo! a cross of silver swung.

Well she knew its graven sign,
Squando's bird and totem pine;
And, a mirage of the brain,
Flowed her childhood back again.

Flashed the roof the sunshine through,
Into space the walls outgrew;
On the Indian's wigwam-mat,
Blossom-crowned, again she sat.

Cool she felt the west wind blow,
In her ear the pines sang low,
And, like links from out a chain,
Dropped the years of care and pain.

From the outward toil and din,
From the griefs that gnaw within,
To the freedom of the woods
Called the birds, and winds, and floods.

Well, oh, painful minister!
Watch thy flock, but blame not her,
If her ear grew sharp to hear
All their voices whispering near.

Blame her not, as to her soul
All the desert's glamour stole,
That a tear for childhood's loss
Dropped upon the Indian's cross.

When, that night, the Book was read,
And she bowed her widowed head,
And a prayer for each loved name
Rose like incense from a flame

To the listening ear of Heaven,
Lo! another name was given:
"Father, give the Indian rest!
Bless him! for his love has blest!"

MY PLAYMATE.

The pines were dark on Ramoth hill,
   Their song was soft and low;
The blossoms in the sweet May wind
   Were falling like the snow.

The blossoms drifted at our feet,
   The orchard birds sang clear;
The sweetest and the saddest day
   It seemed of all the year.

For, more to me than birds or flowers,
   My playmate left her home,
And took with her the laughing spring,
   The music and the bloom.

She kissed the lips of kith and kin,
   She laid her hand in mine:
What more could ask the bashful boy
   Who fed her father's kine?

MY PLAYMATE.

She left us in the bloom of May:
    The constant years told o'er
Their seasons with as sweet May morns,
    But she came back no more.

I walk, with noiseless feet, the round
    Of uneventful years;
Still o'er and o'er I sow the spring
    And reap the autumn ears.

She lives where all the golden year
    Her summer roses blow;
The dusky children of the sun
    Before her come and go.

There haply with her jewelled hands
    She smooths her silken gown, —
No more the homespun lap wherein
    I shook the walnuts down.

The wild grapes wait us by the brook,
    The brown nuts on the hill,
And still the May-day flowers make sweet
    The woods of Follymill.

The lilies blossom in the pond,
    The bird builds in the tree,
The dark pines sing on Ramoth hill
    The slow song of the sea.

I wonder if she thinks of them,
    And how the old time seems, —
If ever the pines of Ramoth wood
    Are sounding in her dreams.

I see her face, I hear her voice:
    Does she remember mine?
And what to her is now the boy
    Who fed her father's kine?

What cares she that the orioles build
    For other eyes than ours, —
That other hands with nuts are filled,
    And other laps with flowers?

O playmate in the golden time!
    Our mossy seat is green,
Its fringing violets blossom yet,
    The old trees o'er it lean.

The winds so sweet with birch and fern
   A sweeter memory blow;
And there in spring the veeries sing
   The song of long ago.

And still the pines of Ramoth wood
   Are moaning like the sea, —
The moaning of the sea of change
   Between myself and thee!

POEMS AND LYRICS.

THE SHADOW AND THE LIGHT.

"And I sought whence is Evil: I set before the eye of my spirit the whole creation; whatsoever we see therein — sea, earth, air, stars, trees, mortal creatures, — yea, whatsoever there is we do not see — angels and spiritual powers. Where is evil, and whence comes it, since God the Good hath created all things? Why made He anything at all of evil, and not rather by His All-mightiness cause it not to be? These thoughts I turned in my miserable heart, overcharged with most gnawing cares." "And, admonished to return to myself, I entered even into my inmost soul, Thou being my guide, and beheld even beyond my soul and mind the Light unchangeable. He who knows the Truth knows what that Light is, and he that knows it knows Eternity! O Truth, who art Eternity! Love, who art Truth! Eternity, who art Love! And I beheld that Thou madest all things good, and to Thee is nothing whatsoever evil. From the angel to the worm, from the first motion to the last, Thou settest each in its place, and everything is good in its kind. Woe is me! — how high art Thou in the highest, how deep in the deepest! and Thou never departest from us, and we scarcely return to Thee." — AUGUSTINE'S SOLILOQUIES, Book vii.

THE fourteen centuries fall away
 Between us and the Afric saint,
 And at his side we urge, to-day,
The immemorial quest and old complaint.

THE SHADOW AND THE LIGHT.

No outward sign to us is given, —
    From sea or earth comes no reply;
  Hushed as the warm Numidian heaven
He vainly questioned bends our frozen sky.

  No victory comes of all our strife, —
    From all we grasp the meaning slips;
  The Sphinx sits at the gate of life,
With the old question on her awful lips.

  In paths unknown we hear the feet
    Of fear before, and guilt behind:
  We pluck the wayside fruit, and eat
Ashes and dust beneath its golden rind.

  From age to age descends unchecked
    The sad bequest of sire to son,
  The body's taint, the mind's defect —
Through every web of life the dark threads run

  Oh! why and whither? — God knows all:
    I only know that he is good,

And that whatever may befall
Or here or there, must be the best that could.

Between the dreadful cherubim
    A Father's face I still discern,
  As Moses looked of old on him,
And saw his glory into goodness turn!

For he is merciful as just:
    And so, by faith correcting sight,
  I bow before his will, and trust
Howe'er they seem he doeth all things right.

And dare to hope that he will make
    The rugged smooth, the doubtful plain;
  His mercy never quite forsake;
His healing visit every realm of pain;

That suffering is not his revenge
    Upon his creatures weak and frail,
  Sent on a pathway new and strange
With feet that wander and with eyes that fail;

That, o'er the crucible of pain,
    Watches the tender eye of Love
The slow transmuting of the chain
Whose links are iron below to gold above!

Ah, me! we doubt the shining skies
    Seen through our shadows of offence,
And drown with our poor childish cries
The cradle-hymn of kindly Providence.

And still we love the evil cause,
    And of the just effect complain;
We tread upon life's broken laws,
And murmur at our self-inflicted pain;

We turn us from the light, and find
    Our spectral shapes before us thrown,
As they who leave the sun behind
Walk in the shadows of themselves alone.

And scarce by will or strength of ours
    We set our faces to the day;
Weak, wavering, blind, the Eternal Powers
Alone can turn us from ourselves away.

Our weakness is the strength of sin,
    But love must needs be stronger far,
Outreaching all and gathering in
The erring spirit and the wandering star.

A Voice grows with the growing years,
    Earth, hushing down her bitter cry,
Looks upward from her graves, and hears,
"The Resurrection and the Life am I."

Oh, Love Divine! — whose constant beam
    Shines on the eyes that will not see,
And waits to bless us, while we dream
Thou leavest us because we turn from thee!

All souls that struggle and aspire,
    All hearts of prayer by thee are lit;
And, dim or clear, thy tongues of fire
On dusky tribes and twilight centuries sit.

Nor bounds, nor clime, nor creed thou know'st,
    Wide as our need thy favors fall;
The white wings of the Holy Ghost
Stoop, seen or unseen, o'er the heads of all.

Oh, Beauty, old yet ever new! *
　Eternal Voice, and Inward Word.
The Logos of the Greek and Jew,
The old sphere-music which the Samian heard!

Truth which the sage and prophet saw,
　Long sought without but found within,
The Law of Love beyond all law,
The Life o'erflooding mortal death and sin!

Shine on us with the light which glowed
　Upon the trance-bound shepherd's way,
Who saw the Darkness overflowed
And drowned by tides of everlasting Day.†

---

* "Too late I loved Thee, O Beauty of ancient days, yet ever new! And lo! Thou wert within, and I abroad searching for Thee. Thou wert with me, but I was not with Thee."— AUGUST. SOLILOQ., Book x.

† "And I saw that there was an Ocean of Darkness and Death: but an infinite Ocean of Light and Love flowed over the Ocean of Darkness: And in that I saw the infinite Love of God."— GEORGE FOX'S JOURNAL.

Shine, light of God! — make broad thy scope
    To all who sin and suffer; more
And better than we dare to hope
With Heaven's compassion make our longings poor!

THE GIFT OF TRITEMIUS.

Tritemius of Herbipolis, one day,
While kneeling at the altar's foot to pray,
Alone with God, as was his pious choice,
Heard from without a miserable voice,
A sound which seemed of all sad things to tell,
As of a lost soul crying out of hell.

Thereat the Abbot paused; the chain whereby
His thoughts went upward broken by that cry;
And, looking from the casement, saw below
A wretched woman, with gray hair a-flow,
And withered hands held up to him, who cried
For alms as one who might not be denied.

She cried, "For the dear love of Him who gave
His life for ours, my child from bondage save,—

My beautiful, brave first-born, chained with slaves
In the Moor's galley, where the sun-smit waves
Lap the white walls of Tunis!"—"What I can
I give," Tritemius said: "my prayers."—"O, man
Of God!" she cried, for grief had made her bold,
"Mock me not thus: I ask not prayers, but gold.
Words will not serve me, alms alone suffice:
Even while I speak perchance my first-born dies."

"Woman!" Tritemius answered, "from our door
None go unfed: hence are we always poor:
A single soldo is our only store.
Thou hast our prayers;—what can we give thee
    more?"

"Give me," she said, "the silver candlesticks
On either side of the great crucifix.
God well may spare them on his errands sped,
Or he can give you golden ones instead."

Then spake Tritemius, "Even as thy word,
Woman, so be it! (Our most gracious Lord,

Who loveth mercy more than sacrifice,
Pardon me if a human soul I prize
Above the gifts upon his altar piled!)
Take what thou askest, and redeem thy child."

But his hand trembled as the holy alms
He placed within the beggar's eager palms;
And as she vanished down the linden shade,
He bowed his head and for forgiveness prayed.

So the day passed, and when the twilight came
He woke to find the chapel all a-flame,
And, dumb with grateful wonder, to behold
Upon the altar candlesticks of gold!

THE EVE OF ELECTION.

    From gold to gray
    Our mild sweet day
Of Indian Summer fades too soon;
    But tenderly
    Above the sea
Hangs, white and calm, the Hunter's moon.

    In its pale fire,
    The village spire
Shows like the zodiac's spectral lance;
    The painted walls
    Whereon it falls
Transfigured stand in marble trance!

O'er fallen leaves
The west wind grieves,
Yet comes a seed-time round again;
And morn shall see
The State sown free
With baleful tares or healthful grain.

Along the street
The shadows meet
Of Destiny, whose hands conceal
The moulds of fate
That shape the State,
And make or mar the common weal.

Around I see
The powers that be;
I stand by Empire's primal springs;
And princes meet
In every street,
And hear the tread of uncrowned kings!

THE EVE OF ELECTION.

    Hark! through the crowd
    The laugh runs loud,
Beneath the sad, rebuking moon.
    God save the land,
    A careless hand
May shake or swerve ere morrow's noon!

    No jest is this;
    One cast amiss
May blast the hope of Freedom's year.
    Oh, take me where
    Are hearts of prayer,
And foreheads bowed in reverent fear!

    Not lightly fall
    Beyond recall
The written scrolls a breath can float;
    The crowning fact,
    The kingliest act
Of Freedom, is the freeman's vote!

THE EVE OF ELECTION.

    For pearls that gem
      A diadem
The diver in the deep sea dies:
    The regal right
    We boast to-night
Is ours through costlier sacrifice:

    The blood of Vane,
    His prison pain
Who traced the path the Pilgrim trod,
    And hers whose faith
    Drew strength from death,
And prayed her Russell up to God!

    Our hearts grow cold,
    We lightly hold
A right which brave men died to gain;
    The stake, the cord,
    The axe, the sword,
Grim nurses at its birth of pain.

The shadow rend,
And o'er us bend,
Oh, martyrs, with your crowns and palms, —
Breathe through these throngs
Your battle songs,
Your scaffold prayers, and dungeon psalms!

Look from the sky,
Like God's great eye,
Thou solemn moon, with searching beam;
Till in the sight
Of thy pure light
Our mean self-seekings meaner seem.

Shame from our hearts
Unworthy arts,
The fraud designed, the purpose dark;
And smite away
The hands we lay
Profanely on the sacred ark.

To party claims,
And private aims,
Reveal that august face of Truth,
Whereto are given
The age of heaven,
The beauty of immortal youth.

So shall our voice
Of sovereign choice
Swell the deep bass of duty done,
And strike the key
Of time to be,
When God and man shall speak as one!

THE OVER-HEART.

For of Him, and through Him, and to Him are all things, to whom be glory for ever! PAUL.

ABOVE, below, in sky and sod,
   In leaf and spar, in star and man,
   Well might the wise Athenian scan
The geometric signs of God,
   The measured order of his plan.

And India's mystics sang aright
   Of the One Life pervading all, —
   One Being's tidal rise and fall
In soul and form, in sound and sight, —
   Eternal outflow and recall.

God is: and man in guilt and fear
   The central fact of Nature owns; —
   Kneels, trembling, by his altar-stones,
And darkly dreams the ghastly smear
   Of blood appeases and atones.

Guilt shapes the Terror: deep within
    The human heart the secret lies
    Of all the hideous deities;
And, painted on a ground of sin,
    The fabled gods of torment rise!

And what is He? — The ripe grain nods,
    The sweet dews fall, the sweet flowers blow;
    But darker signs his presence show:
The earthquake and the storm are God's,
    And good and evil interflow.

Oh, hearts of love! Oh, souls that turn
    Like sunflowers to the pure and best!
    To you the truth is manifest:
For they the mind of Christ discern
    Who lean like John upon his breast!

In him of whom the Sybil told,
    For whom the prophet's harp was toned,
    Whose need the sage and magian owned,
The loving heart of God behold,
    The hope for which the ages groaned!

Fade, pomp of dreadful imagery
    Wherewith mankind have deified
    Their hate, and selfishness, and pride!
Let the scared dreamer wake to see
    The Christ of Nazareth at his side!

What doth that holy Guide require? —
    No rite of pain, nor gift of blood,
    But man a kindly brotherhood,
Looking, where duty is desire,
    To him, the beautiful and good.

Gone be the faithlessness of fear,
    And let the pitying heaven's sweet rain
    Wash out the altar's bloody stain;
The law of Hatred disappear,
    The law of Love alone remain.

How fall the idols false and grim! —
    And lo! their hideous wreck above
    The emblems of the Lamb and Dove!
Man turns from God, not God from him;
    And guilt, in suffering, whispers Love!

The world sits at the feet of Christ,
    Unknowing, blind, and unconsoled;
    It yet shall touch his garment's fold,
And feel the heavenly Alchemist
    Transform its very dust to gold.

The theme befitting angel tongues
    Beyond a mortal's scope has grown.
    Oh, heart of mine! with reverence own
The fullness which to it belongs,
    And trust the unknown for the known!

IN REMEMBRANCE OF JOSEPH STURGE.

In the fair land o'erwatched by Ischia's mountains,
    Across the charmèd bay
Whose blue waves keep with Capri's silver fountains
    Perpetual holiday,

A king lies dead, his wafer duly eaten,
    His gold-bought masses given;
And Rome's great altar smokes with gums to sweeten
    Her foulest gift to Heaven.

And while all Naples thrills with mute thanksgiving,
    The court of England's queen
For the dead monster so abhorred while living
    In mourning garb is seen.

With a true sorrow God rebukes that feigning:
    By lone Edgbaston's side
Stands a great city in the sky's sad raining,
    Bare-headed and wet-eyed!

Silent for once the restless hive of labor,
    Save the low funeral tread,
Or voice of craftsman whispering to his neighbor
    The good deeds of the dead.

For him no minster's chant of the immortals
    Rose from the lips of sin;
No mitred priest swung back the heavenly portals
    To let the white soul in.

But Age and Sickness framed their tearful faces
    In the low hovel's door,
And prayers went up from all the dark by-places
    And Ghettos of the poor.

The pallid toiler and the negro chattel,
    The vagrant of the street,
The human dice wherewith in games of battle
    The lords of earth compete,

Touched with a grief that needs no outward draping,
    All swelled the long lament
Of grateful hearts, instead of marble, shaping
    His viewless monument!

For never yet, with ritual pomp and splendor,
    In the long heretofore,
A heart more loyal, warm, and true, and tender,
    Has England's turf closed o'er.

And if there fell from out her grand old steeples
    No crash of brazen wail,
The murmurous woe of kindreds, tongues, and peoples
    Swept in on every gale.

It came from Holstein's birchen-belted meadows,
    And from the tropic calms
Of Indian islands in the sun-smit shadows
    Of Occidental palms;

From the locked roadsteads of the Bothnian peasants,
    And harbors of the Finn,
Where war's worn victims saw his gentle presence
    Come sailing, Christ-like, in,

To seek the lost, to build the old waste-places,
    To link the hostile shores
Of severing seas, and sow with England's daisies
    The moss of Finland's moors.

Thanks for the good man's beautiful example,
    Who in the vilest saw
Some sacred crypt or altar of a temple
    Still vocal with God's law;

And heard with tender ear the spirit sighing
    As from its prison cell,
Praying for pity, like the mournful crying
    Of Jonah out of hell.

Not his the golden pen's or lip's persuasion,
    But a fine sense of right,
And truth's directness, meeting each occasion
    Straight as a line of light.

His faith and works, like streams that intermingle,
    In the same channel ran:
The crystal clearness of an eye kept single
    Shamed all the frauds of man.

The very gentlest of all human natures
    He joined to courage strong,
And love outreaching unto all God's creatures
    With sturdy hate of wrong

Tender as woman: manliness and meekness
    In him were so allied
That they who judged him by his strength or weakness
    Saw but a single side.

Men failed, betrayed him, but his zeal seemed nourished
    By failure and by fall;
Still a large faith in human kind he cherished,
    And in God's love for all.

And now he rests: his greatness and his sweetness
    No more shall seem at strife;
And death has moulded into calm completeness
    The statue of his life.

Where the dews glisten and the song-birds warble,
    His dust to dust is laid,
In Nature's keeping, with no pomp of marble
    To shame his modest shade.

The forges glow, the hammers all are ringing;
    Beneath its smoky vail,
Hard by, the city of his love is swinging
    Its clamorous iron flail.

But round his grave are quietude and beauty,
  And the sweet heaven above, —
The fitting symbols of a life of duty
  Transfigured into love!

TRINITAS.

At morn I prayed, "I fain would see
How Three are One, and One is Three.
Read the dark riddle unto me."

I wandered forth, the sun and air
I saw bestowed with equal care
On good and evil, foul and fair.

No partial favor dropped the rain; —
Alike the righteous and profane
Rejoiced above their heading grain.

And my heart murmured, "Is it meet
That blindfold Nature thus should treat
With equal hand the tares and wheat?"

A presence melted through my mood, —
A warmth, a light, a sense of good,
Like sunshine through a winter wood.

I saw that presence, mailed complete
In her white innocence, pause to greet
A fallen sister of the street.

Upon her bosom snowy pure
The lost one clung, as if secure
From inward guilt or outward lure.

"Beware!" I said; "in this I see
No gain to her, but loss to thee:
Who touches pitch defiled must be."

I passed the haunts of shame and sin,
And a voice whispered, "Who therein
Shall these lost souls to Heaven's peace win?

"Who there shall hope and health dispense,
And lift the ladder up from thence
Whose rounds are prayers of penitence?"

I said, "No higher life they know;
These earth-worms love to have it so.
Who stoops to raise them sinks as low."

That night with painful care I read
What Hippo's saint and Calvin said, —
The living seeking to the dead!

In vain I turned, in weary quest,
Old pages, where (God give them rest!)
The poor creed-mongers dreamed and guessed.

And still I prayed, "Lord, let me see
How Three are One, and One is Three;
Read the dark riddle unto me!"

Then something whispered, "Dost thou pray
For what thou hast? This very day
The Holy Three have crossed thy way.

"Did not the gifts of sun and air
To good and ill alike declare
The all-compassionate Father's care?

"In the white soul that stooped to raise
The lost one from her evil ways,
Thou saw'st the Christ, whom angels praise!

"A bodiless Divinity,
The still, small Voice that spake to thee
Was the Holy Spirit's mystery!

"Oh, blind of sight, of faith how small!
Father, and Son, and Holy Call;—
This day thou hast denied them all!

"Revealed in love and sacrifice,
The Holiest passed before thine eyes,
One and the same, in threefold guise.

"The equal Father in rain and sun,
His Christ in the good to evil done,
His Voice in thy soul;—and the Three are One!"

I shut my grave Aquinas fast;
The monkish gloss of ages past,
The schoolman's creed aside I cast.

And my heart answered, "Lord, I see
How Three are One, and One is Three;
Thy riddle hath been read to me!"

THE OLD BURYING-GROUND.

Our vales are sweet with fern and rose,
   Our hills are maple-crowned;
But not from them our fathers chose
   The village burying-ground.

The dreariest spot in all the land
   To Death they set apart;
With scanty grace from Nature's hand,
   And none from that of Art.

A winding wall of mossy stone,
   Frost-flung and broken, lines
A lonesome acre thinly grown
   With grass and wandering vines.

Without the wall a birch-tree shows
   Its drooped and tasselled head;
Within, a stag-horned sumach grows,
   Fern-leafed, with spikes of red.

There, sheep that graze the neighboring plain
   Like white ghosts come and go,
The farm-horse drags his fetlock chain,
   The cow-bell tinkles slow.

Low moans the river from its bed,
   The distant pines reply;
Like mourners shrinking from the dead,
   They stand apart and sigh.

Unshaded smites the summer sun,
   Unchecked the winter blast;
The school-girl learns the place to shun,
   With glances backward cast.

For thus our fathers testified —
   That he might read who ran —
The emptiness of human pride,
   The nothingness of man.

They dared not plant the grave with **flowers,**
   Nor dress the funeral sod,
Where, with a love as deep as ours,
   They left their dead with God.

The hard and thorny path they kept
   From beauty turned aside;
Nor missed they over those who slept
   The grace to life denied.

Yet still the wilding flowers would blow,
   The golden leaves would fall,
The seasons come, the seasons go,
   And God be good to all.

Above the graves the blackberry hung,
   In bloom and green its wreath,
And harebells swung as if they rung
   The chimes of peace beneath.

The beauty Nature loves to share,
   The gifts she hath for all,
The common light, the common air,
   O'ercrept the graveyard's wall.

It knew the glow of eventide,
   The sunrise and the noon,
And glorified and sanctified
   It slept beneath the moon.

With flowers or snow-flakes for its sod,
   Around the seasons ran,
And evermore the love of God
   Rebuked the fear of man.

We dwell with fears on either hand,
   Within a daily strife,
And spectral problems waiting stand
   Before the gates of life.

The doubts we vainly seek to solve,
   The truths we know, are one;
The known and nameless stars revolve
   Around the Central Sun.

And if we reap as we have sown,
   And take the dole we deal,
The law of pain is love alone,
   The wounding is to heal.

Unharmed from change to change we glide,
   We fall as in our dreams;
The far-off terror at our side
   A smiling angel seems.

Secure on God's all-tender heart
   Alike rest great and small:
Why fear to lose our little part,
   When he is pledged for all?

O fearful heart and troubled brain!
   Take hope and strength from this, —
That Nature never hints in vain,
   Nor prophesies amiss.

Her wild birds sing the same sweet stave,
   Her lights and airs are given
Alike to playground and the grave;
   And over both is Heaven.

THE PIPES AT LUCKNOW.

Pipes of the misty moorlands,
    Voice of the glens and hills;
The droning of the torrents,
    The treble of the rills!
Not the braes of broom and heather,
    Nor the mountains dark with rain,
Nor maiden bower, nor border tower
    Have heard your sweetest strain!

Dear to the Lowland reaper,
    And plaided mountaineer,—
To the cottage and the castle
    The Scottish pipes are dear;—
Sweet sounds the ancient pibroch
    O'er mountain, loch, and glade;
But the sweetest of all music
    The Pipes at Lucknow played.

Day by day the Indian tiger
  Louder yelled, and nearer crept;
Round and round the jungle-serpent
  Near and nearer circles swept.
"Pray for rescue, wives and mothers, —
  Pray to-day!" the soldier said;
"To-morrow, death's between us
  And the wrong and shame we dread."

Oh! they listened, looked, and waited,
  Till their hope became despair;
And the sobs of low bewailing
  Filled the pauses of their prayer.
Then up spake a Scottish maiden,
  With her ear unto the ground:
"Dinna ye hear it? — dinna ye hear it?
  The pipes o' Havelock sound!"

Hushed the wounded man his groaning;
  Hushed the wife her little ones;
Alone they heard the drum-roll
  And the roar of Sepoy guns.

But to sounds of home and childhood
    The Highland ear was true; —
As her mother's cradle-crooning
    The mountain pipes she knew.

Like the march of soundless music
    Through the vision of the seer,
More of feeling than of hearing,
    Of the heart than of the ear,
She knew the droning pibroch,
    She knew the Campbell's call:
"Hark! hear ye no' MacGregor's, —
    The grandest o' them all!"

Oh! they listened, dumb and breathless,
    And they caught the sound at last:
Faint and far beyond the Goomtee
    Rose and fell the piper's blast!
Then a burst of wild thanksgiving
    Mingled woman's voice and man's;
"God be praised! — the march of Havelock!
    The piping of the clans!"

Louder, nearer, fierce as vengeance,
　　Sharp and shrill as swords at strife,
Came the wild MacGregor's clan-call,
　　Stinging all the air to life.
But when the far-off dust cloud
　　To plaided legions grew,
Full tenderly and blithesomely
　　The pipes of rescue blew!

Round the silver domes of Lucknow,
　　Moslem mosque and Pagan shrine,
Breathed the air to Britons dearest,
　　The air of Auld Lang Syne.
O'er the cruel roll of war-drums
　　Rose that sweet and homelike strain;
And the tartan clove the turban,
　　As the Goomtee cleaves the plain.

Dear to the corn-land reaper
　　And plaided mountaineer,—
To the cottage and the castle
　　The piper's song is dear.

Sweet sounds the Gaelic pibroch
    O'er mountain, glen, and glade,
But the sweetest of all music
    The Pipes at Lucknow played!

MY PSALM.

I mourn no more my vanished years:
    Beneath a tender rain,
An April rain of smiles and tears,
    My heart is young again.

The west winds blow, and, singing low,
    I hear the glad streams run;
The windows of my soul I throw
    Wide open to the sun.

No longer forward nor behind
    I look in hope or fear;
But, grateful, take the good I find,
    The best of now and here.

I plough no more a desert land,
    To harvest weed and tare;
The manna dropping from God's hand
    Rebukes my painful care.

I break my pilgrim staff, — I lay
    Aside the toiling oar;
The angel sought so far away
    I welcome at my door.

The airs of Spring may never play
    Among the ripening corn,
Nor freshness of the flowers of May
    Blow through the Autumn morn;

Yet shall the blue-eyed gentian look
    Through fringéd lids to heaven,
And the pale aster in the brook
    Shall see its image given; —

The woods shall wear their robes of praise,
    The south wind softly sigh,
And sweet, calm days in golden haze
    Melt down the amber sky.

Not less shall manly deed and word
    Rebuke an age of wrong;
The graven flowers that wreathe the sword
    Make not the blade less strong.

But smiting hands shall learn to heal, —
    To build as to destroy;
Nor less my heart for others feel
    That I the more enjoy.

All as God wills, who wisely heeds
    To give or to withhold,
And knoweth more of all my needs
    Than all my prayers have told!

Enough that blessings undeserved
    Have marked my erring track: —
That wheresoe'er my feet have swerved,
    His chastening turned me back: —

That more and more a Providence
    Of love is understood,
Making the springs of time and sense
    Sweet with eternal good;

That death seems but a covered way
    Which opens into light,
Wherein no blinded child can stray
    Beyond the Father's sight; —

That care and trial seem at last,
    Through Memory's sunset air,
Like mountain-ranges overpast,
    In purple distance fair; —

That all the jarring notes of life
    Seem blending in a psalm,
And all the angles of its strife
    Slow rounding into calm.

And so the shadows fall apart,
    And so the west winds play;
And all the windows of my heart
    I open to the day.

LE MARAIS DU CYGNE.*

A BLUSH as of roses
    Where rose never grew!
Great drops on the bunch-grass,
    But not of the dew!
A taint in the sweet air
    For wild bees to shun!
A stain that shall never
    Bleach out in the sun!

Back, steed of the prairies!
    Sweet song-bird, fly back!
Wheel hither, bald vulture!
    Gray wolf, call thy pack!

---

* The massacre of unarmed and unoffending men, in Southern Kansas, took place near the Marais du Cygne of the French *voyageurs*.

The foul human vultures
    Have feasted and fled;
The wolves of the Border
    Have crept from the dead.

From the hearths of their cabins,
    The fields of their corn,
Unwarned and unweaponed,
    The victims were torn, —
By the whirlwind of murder
    Swooped up and swept on
To the low, reedy fen-lands,
    The Marsh of the Swan.

With a vain plea for mercy
    No stout knee was crooked:
In the mouths of the rifles
    Right manly they looked.
How paled the May sunshine,
    O, Marais du Cygne!
On death for the strong life,
    On red grass for green!

In the homes of their rearing,
    Yet warm with their lives,
Ye wait the dead only,
    Poor children and wives!
Put out the red forge-fire,
    The smith shall not come;
Unyoke the brown oxen,
    The ploughman lies dumb.

Wind slow from the Swan's Marsh,
    O dreary death train,
With pressed lips as bloodless
    As lips of the slain!
Kiss down the young eyelids,
    Smooth down the gray hairs;
Let tears quench the curses
    That burn through your prayers.

Strong man of the prairies,
    Mourn bitter and wild!
Wail, desolate woman!
    Weep, fatherless child!

But the grain of God springs up
   From ashes beneath,
And the crown of his harvest
   Is life out of death.

Not in vain on the dial
   The shade moves along,
To point the great contrasts
   Of right and of wrong:
Free homes and free altars,
   Free prairie and flood, —
The reeds of the Swan's Marsh,
   Whose bloom is of blood!

On the lintels of Kansas
   That blood shall not dry;
Henceforth the Bad Angel
   Shall harmless go by;
Henceforth to the sunset,
   Unchecked on her way,
Shall Liberty follow
   The march of the day.

"THE ROCK" IN EL GHOR.

Dead Petra in her hill-tomb sleeps,
    Her stones of emptiness remain;
Around her sculptured mystery sweeps
    The lonely waste of Edom's plain.

From the doomed dwellers in the cleft
    The bow of vengeance turns not back;
Of all her myriads none are left
    Along the Wady Mousa's track.

Clear in the hot Arabian day
    Her arches spring, her statues climb;
Unchanged, the graven wonders pay
    No tribute to the spoiler, Time!

Unchanged the awful lithograph
    Of power and glory undertrod, —
Of nations scattered like the chaff
    Blown from the threshing-floor of God.

Yet shall the thoughtful stranger turn
    From Petra's gates, with deeper awe
To mark afar the burial urn
    Of Aaron on the cliffs of Hor;

And where upon its ancient guard
    Thy Rock, El Ghor, is standing yet, —
Looks from its turrets desertward,
    And keeps the watch that God has set;

The same as when in thunders loud
    It heard the voice of God to man, —
As when it saw in fire and cloud
    The angels walk in Israel's van!

Or when from Ezion-Geber's way
    It saw the long procession file,
And heard the Hebrew timbrels play
    The music of the lordly Nile;

Or saw the tabernacle pause,
    Cloud-bound, by Kadesh Barnea's wells,
While Moses graved the sacred laws,
    And Aaron swung his golden bells.

Rock of the desert, prophet-sung!
    How grew its shadowing pile at length,
A symbol, in the Hebrew tongue,
    Of God's eternal love and strength.

On lip of bard and scroll of seer,
    From age to age went down the name,
Until the Shiloh's promised year,
    And Christ, the Rock of Ages, came!

The path of life we walk to-day
    Is strange as that the Hebrews trod:
We need the shadowing rock, as they, —
    We need, like them, the guides of God.

God send his angels, Cloud and Fire,
    To lead us o'er the desert sand!
God give our hearts their long desire, —
    His shadow in a weary land!

ON A PRAYER-BOOK,

WITH ITS FRONTISPIECE, ARY SCHEFFER'S "CHRISTUS CONSOLATOR," AMERICAN-
IZED BY THE OMISSION OF THE BLACK MAN.

O, ARY SCHEFFER! when beneath thine eye,
   Touched with the light that cometh from above,
   Grew the sweet picture of the dear Lord's love,
No dream hadst thou that Christian hands would tear
Therefrom the token of his equal care,
   And make thy symbol of his truth a lie!
The poor, dumb slave whose shackles fall away
   In his compassionate gaze, grubbed smoothly out,
   To mar no more the exercise devout
Of sleek oppression kneeling down to pray
Where the great oriel stains the Sabbath day!
Let whoso can before such praying books
   Kneel on his velvet cushions; I, for one,
   Would sooner bow, a Parsee, to the sun,
Or tend a prayer-wheel in Thibetan brooks,

Or beat a drum on Yedo's temple-floor.
No falser idol man has bowed before,
In Indian groves or islands of the sea,
    Than that which through the quaint-carved Gothic door
Looks forth,—a Church without humanity!
    Patron of pride, and prejudice, and wrong,—
    The rich man's charm and fetish of the strong,
The Eternal Fullness meted, clipped, and shorn,
The seamless robe of equal mercy torn,
The dear Christ hidden from his kindred flesh,
And, in his poor ones, crucified afresh!
Better the simple Lama scattering wide,
    Where sweeps the storm Alechan's steppes along,
His paper horses for the lost to ride,
And wearying Buddha with his prayers to make
The figures living for the traveller's sake,
Than he who hopes with cheap praise to beguile
The ear of God, dishonoring man the while:
Who dreams the pearl gate's hinges, rusty grown,
Are moved by flattery's oil of tongue alone;
That in the scale Eternal Justice bears

The generous deed weighs less than selfish prayers,
And words intoned with graceful unction move
The Eternal Goodness more than lives of truth and
    love.

Alas, the Church! — The reverend head of Jay,
  Enhaloed with its saintly silvered hair,
  Adorns no more the places of her prayer;
And brave young Tyng, too early called away,
  Troubles the Haman of her courts no more
  Like the just Hebrew at th' Assyrian's door;
  And her sweet ritual, beautiful but dead
  As the dry husk from which the grain is shed,
  And holy hymns from which the life devout
Of saints and martyrs has well-nigh gone out,
    Like candles dying in exhausted air,
For Sabbath use in measured grists are ground;
And, ever while the spiritual mill goes round,
Between the upper and the nether stones,
  Unseen, unheard, the wretched bondman groans,
And urges his vain plea, prayer-smothered, anthem-
    drowned!

Oh, heart of mine, keep patience! — Looking forth,
   As from the Mount of Vision, I behold,
Pure, just, and free, the Church of Christ on earth, —
   The martyr's dream, the golden age foretold!
And found, at last, the mystic Graal I see
   Brimmed with His blessing, pass from lip to lip
   In sacred pledge of human fellowship:
   And over all the songs of angels hear, —
   Songs of the love that casteth out all fear, —
   Songs of the Gospel of Humanity!
   Lo! in the midst, with the same look he wore,
   Healing and blessing on Genesaret's shore,
   Folding together, with the all-tender might
Of his great love, the dark hands and the white,
   Stands the Consoler, soothing every pain,
Making all burdens light, and breaking every chain!

TO J. T. F.

(ON A BLANK LEAF OF "POEMS PRINTED, NOT PUBLISHED.")

WELL thought! who would not rather hear
The songs to Love and Friendship sung
Than those which move the stranger's tongue,
And feed his unselected ear?

Our social joys are more than fame;
Life withers in the public look.
Why mount the pillory of a book,
Or barter comfort for a name?

Who in a house of glass would dwell,
With curious eyes at every pane?
To ring him in and out again,
Who wants the public crier's bell?

To see the angel in one's way,
Who wants to play the ass's part, —
Bear on his back the wizard Art,
And in his service speak or bray?

And who his manly locks would shave,
And quench the eyes of common sense,
To share the noisy recompense
That mocked the shorn and blinded slave?

The heart has needs beyond the head,
And, starving in the plenitude
Of strange gifts, craves its common food, —
Our human nature's daily bread.

We are but men: no gods are we,
To sit in mid-heaven, cold and bleak,
Each separate, on his painful peak,
Thin-cloaked in self-complacency!

Better his lot whose axe is swung
In Wartburg woods: or that poor girl's
Who by the Ilm her spindle whirls
And sings the songs that Luther sung,

Than his who, old, and cold, and vain,
At Weimar sat, a demigod,
And bowed with Jove's imperial nod
His votaries in and out again!

TO J. T. F.

Ply, Vanity, thy wingéd feet!
Ambition, hew thy rocky stair!
Who envies him who feeds on air
The icy splendor of his seat?

I see your Alps, above me, cut
The dark, cold sky; and dim and lone
I see ye sitting — stone on stone —
With human senses dulied and shut.

I could not reach you, if I would,
Nor sit among your cloudy shapes;
And (spare the fable of the grapes
And fox) I would not if I could.

Keep to your lofty pedestals!
The safer plain below I choose:
Who never wins can rarely lose,
Who never climbs as rarely falls.

Let such as love the eagle's scream
Divide with him his home of ice:
For me shall gentler notes suffice, —
The valley-song of bird and stream;

The pastoral bleat, the drone of bees,
The flail-beat chiming far away,
The cattle-low, at shut of day,
The voice of God in leaf and breeze!

Then lend thy hand, my wiser friend,
And help me to the vales below
(In truth, I have not far to go,)
Where sweet with flowers the fields extend.

THE PALM-TREE.

Is it the palm, the cocoa-palm,
On the Indian Sea, by the isles of balm?
Or is it a ship in the breezeless calm?

A ship whose keel is of palm beneath,
Whose ribs of palm have a palm-bark sheath,
And a rudder of palm it steereth with.

Branches of palm are its spars and rails,
Fibres of palm are its woven sails,
And the rope is of palm that idly trails!

What does the good ship bear so well?
The cocoa-nut with its stony shell,
And the milky sap of its inner cell.

What are its jars, so smooth and fine,
But hollowed nuts, filled with oil and wine,
And the cabbage that ripens under the Line!

Who smokes his nargileh, cool and calm?
The master, whose cunning and skill could charm
Cargo and ship from the bounteous palm.

In the cabin, he sits on a palm-mat soft,
From a beaker of palm his drink is quaffed,
And a palm-thatch shields from the sun aloft!

His dress is woven of palmy strands,
And he holds a palm-leaf scroll in his hands,
Traced with the Prophet's wise commands!

The turban folded about his head
Was daintily wrought of the palm-leaf braid,
And the fan that cools him of palm was made.

Of threads of palm was the carpet spun
Whereon he kneels when the day is done,
And the foreheads of Islam are bowed as one!

To him the palm is a gift divine,
Wherein all uses of man combine,—
House, and raiment, and food, and wine!

And, in the hour of his great release,
His need of the palm shall only cease
With the shroud wherein he lieth in peace.

"Allah il Allah!" he sings his psalm,
On the Indian Sea, by the isles of balm;
"Thanks to Allah who gives the palm!"

LINES

READ AT THE BOSTON CELEBRATION OF THE HUNDREDTH ANNIVERSARY OF THE BIRTH OF ROBERT BURNS, 25TH 1ST MO., 1859.

How sweetly come the holy psalms
   From saints and martyrs down,
The waving of triumphal palms
   Above the thorny crown!
The choral praise, the chanted prayers
   From harps by angels strung,
The hunted Cameron's mountain airs,
   The hymns that Luther sung!

Yet, jarring not the heavenly notes,
   The sounds of earth are heard,
As through the open minster floats
   The song of breeze and bird!
Not less the wonder of the sky
   That daisies bloom below;
The brook sings on, though loud and high
   The cloudy organs blow!

And, if the tender ear be jarred
    That, haply, hears by turns
The saintly harp of Olney's bard,
    The pastoral pipe of Burns,
No discord mars His perfect plan
    Who gave them both a tongue;
For he who sings the love of man
    The love of God hath sung!

To-day be every fault forgiven
    Of him in whom we joy!
We take, with thanks, the gold of Heaven
    And leave the earth's alloy.
Be ours his music as of Spring,
    His sweetness as of flowers,
The songs the bard himself might sing
    In holier ears than ours.

Sweet airs of love and home, the hum
    Of household melodies,
Come singing, as the robins come
    To sing in door-yard trees.

And, heart to heart, two nations lean,
    No rival wreaths to twine,
But blending in eternal green
    The holly and the pine!

THE RED RIVER VOYAGEUR.

Out and in the river is winding
    The links of its long, red chain
Through belts of dusky pine-land
    And gusty leagues of plain.

Only, at times, a smoke-wreath
    With the drifting cloud-rack joins, —
The smoke of the hunting-lodges
    Of the wild Assiniboins!

Drearily blows the north wind
    From the land of ice and snow;
The eyes that look are weary,
    And heavy the hands that row.

And with one foot on the water,
    And one upon the shore,
The Angel of Shadow gives warning
    That day shall be no more.

Is it the clang of wild-geese?
    Is it the Indian's yell,
That lends to the voice of the north wind
    The tones of a far-off bell?

The voyageur smiles as he listens
    To the sound that grows apace;
Well he knows the vesper ringing
    Of the bells of St. Boniface.

The bells of the Roman Mission,
    That call from their turrets twain,
To the boatman on the river,
    To the hunter on the plain!

Even so in our mortal journey
    The bitter north winds blow,
And thus upon life's Red River
    Our hearts, as oarsmen, row.

And when the Angel of Shadow
    Rests his feet on wave and shore,
And our eyes grow dim with watching
    And our hearts faint at the oar,

Happy is he who heareth
 The signal of his release
In the bells of the Holy City,
 The chimes of eternal peace!

KENOZA LAKE.

As Adam did in Paradise,
    To-day the primal right we claim:
Fair mirror of the woods and skies,
    We give to thee a name.

Lake of the pickerel! — let no more
    The echoes answer back "Great Pond,"
But sweet Kenoza, from thy shore
    And watching hills beyond,

Let Indian ghosts, if such there be
    Who ply unseen their shadowy lines,
Call back the ancient name to thee,
    As with the voice of pines.

The shores we trod as barefoot boys,
    The nutted woods we wandered through,
To friendship, love, and social joys
    We consecrate anew.

Here shall the tender song be sung,
   And memory's dirges soft and low,
And wit shall sparkle on the tongue,
   And mirth shall overflow,

Harmless as summer lightning plays
   From a low, hidden cloud by night,
A light to set the hills ablaze,
   But not a bolt to smite.

In sunny South and prairied West
   Are exiled hearts remembering still,
As bees their hive, as birds their nest,
   The homes of Haverhill.

They join us in our rites to-day;
   And, listening, we may hear, ere long,
From inland lake and ocean bay,
   The echoes of our song.

Kenoza! o'er no sweeter lake
   Shall morning break or noon-cloud sail, —
No fairer face than thine shall take
   The sunset's golden vail.

Long be it ere the tide of trade
  Shall break with harsh-resounding din
The quiet of thy banks of shade,
  And hills that fold thee in.

Still let thy woodlands hide the hare,
  The shy loon sound his trumpet-note;
Wing-weary from his fields of air,
  The wild-goose on thee float.

Thy peace rebuke our feverish stir,
  Thy beauty our deforming strife:
Thy woods and waters minister
  The healing of their life.

And sinless Mirth, from care released,
  Behold, unawed, thy mirrored sky,
Smiling as smiled on Cana's feast
  The Master's loving eye.

And when the summer day grows dim,
  And light mists walk thy mimic sea,
Revive in us the thought of Him
  Who walked on Galilee!

TO G. B. C.

So spake Esaias: so, in words of flame,
Tekoa's prophet-herdsman smote with blame
The traffickers in men, and put to shame,
    All earth and heaven before,
The sacerdotal robbers of the poor.

All the dread Scripture lives for thee again,
To smite like lightning on the hands profane
Lifted to bless the slave-whip and the chain.
    Once more th' old Hebrew tongue
Bends with the shafts of God a bow new strung!

Take up the mantle which the prophets wore;
Warn with their warnings, — show the Christ once more
Bound, scourged, and crucified in his blameless poor:
    And shake above our land
The unquenched bolts that blazed in Hosea's hand!

Not vainly shalt thou cast upon our years
The solemn burdens of the Orient seers,
And smite with truth a guilty nation's ears.
    Mightier was Luther's word
Than Seckingen's mailed arm or Hutton's sword!

THE SISTERS.

A PICTURE BY BARRY.

The shade for me, but over thee
    The lingering sunshine still;
As, smiling, to the silent stream
    Comes down the singing rill,

So come to me, my little one,—
    My years with thee I share,
And mingle with a sister's love
    A mother's tender care.

But keep the smile upon thy lip,
    The trust upon thy brow;
Since for the dear one God hath called
    We have an angel now.

Our mother from the fields of heaven
    Shall still her ear incline:
Nor need we fear her human love
    Is less for love divine.

The songs are sweet they sing beneath
　　The trees of life so fair,
But sweetest of the sounds of heaven
　　Shall be her children's prayer.

Then, darling, rest upon my breast,
　　And teach my heart to lean
With thy sweet trust upon the arm
　　Which folds us both unseen!

LINES

FOR THE AGRICULTURAL AND HORTICULTURAL EXHIBITION AT AMESBURY AND SALISBURY, SEPT. 28, 1858.

This day, two hundred years ago,
  The wild grape by the river's side,
And tasteless ground-nut trailing low,
  The table of the woods supplied.

Unknown the apple's red and gold,
  The blushing tint of peach and pear;
The mirror of the Powow told
  No tale of orchards ripe and rare.

Wild as the fruits he scorned to till,
  These vales the idle Indian trod;
Nor knew the glad, creative skill, —
  The joy of him who toils with God.

O Painter of the fruits and flowers!
  We thank thee for thy wise design
Whereby these human hands of ours
  In Nature's garden work with thine.

And thanks that from our daily need
    The joy of simple faith is born:
That he who smites the summer weed,
    May trust thee for the autumn corn.

Give fools their gold, and knaves their power;
    Let fortune's bubbles rise and fall:
Who sows a field, or trains a flower,
    Or plants a tree, is more than all.

For he who blesses most is blest;
    And God and man shall own his worth
Who toils to leave as his bequest
    An added beauty to the earth.

And, soon or late, to all that sow,
    The time of harvest shall be given;
The flower shall bloom, the fruit shall grow,
    If not on earth, at last in heaven!

THE PREACHER.

Its windows flashing to the sky,
   Beneath a thousand roofs of brown,
Far down the vale, my friend and I
   Beheld the old and quiet town;
The ghostly sails that out at sea
Flapped their white wings of mystery;
The beaches glimmering in the sun,
And the low wooded capes that run
Into the sea-mist north and south;
The sand-bluffs at the river's mouth;
The swinging chain-bridge, and, afar,
The foam-line of the harbor-bar.

Over the woods and meadow-lands
   A crimson-tinted shadow lay
   Of clouds through which the setting day
   Flung a slant glory far away.

It glittered on the wet sea-sands,
    It flamed upon the city's panes,
Smote the white sails of ships that wore
Outward or in, and gilded o'er
    The steeples with their veering vanes!

Awhile my friend with rapid search
    O'erran the landscape. "Yonder spire
    Over gray roofs, a shaft of fire:
What is it, pray?" — "The Whitefield Church!
    Walled about by its basement stones,
    There rest the marvellous prophet's bones."

Then as our homeward way we walked,
Of the great preacher's life we talked;
And through the mystery of our theme
The outward glory seemed to stream,
And Nature's self interpreted
The doubtful record of the dead;
And every level beam that smote
The sails upon the dark afloat

A symbol of the light became
Which touched the shadows of our blame
With tongues of Pentecostal flame.

Over the roofs of the pioneers
Gathers the moss of a hundred years;
On man and his works has passed the change
Which needs must be in a century's range.
The land lies open and warm in the sun,
Anvils clamor and mill-wheels run, —
Flocks on the hill-sides, herds on the plain,
The wilderness gladdened with fruit and grain!
But the living faith of the settlers old
A dead profession their children hold:
To the lust of office and greed of trade
A stepping-stone is the altar made.
The church, to place and power the door,
Rebukes the sin of the world no more,
Nor sees its Lord in the homeless poor.
Everywhere is the grasping hand,
And eager adding of land to land:
And earth, which seemed to the fathers meant
But as a pilgrim's wayside tent, —

A nightly shelter to fold away
When the Lord should call at the break of day, —
Solid and steadfast seems to be,
And Time has forgotten Eternity!

But fresh and green from the rotting roots
Of primal forests the young growth shoots;
From the death of the old the new proceeds,
And the life of truth from the rot of creeds:
On the ladder of God, which upward leads,
The steps of progress are human needs.
For his judgments still are a mighty deep,
And the eyes of his providence never sleep:
When the night is darkest he gives the moon;
When the famine is sorest, the wine and corn!

In the church of the wilderness Edwards wrought,
Shaping his creed at the forge of thought;
And with Thor's own hammer welded and bent
The iron links of his argument,
Which strove to grasp in its mighty span
The purpose of God and the fate of man!

Yet faithful still, in his daily round
To the weak, and the poor, and sin-sick found,
The schoolman's lore and the casuist's art
Drew warmth and life from his fervent heart.
Had he not seen in the solitudes
Of his deep and dark Northampton woods
A vision of love about him fall?
Not the blinding splendor which fell on Saul,
But the tenderer glory that rests on them
Who walk in the New Jerusalem,
Where never the sun nor moon are known,
But the Lord and his love are the light alone!
And watching the sweet, still countenance
Of the wife of his bosom rapt in trance,
Had he not treasured each broken word
Of the mystical wonder seen and heard;
And loved the beautiful dreamer more
That thus to the desert of earth she bore
Clusters of Eschol from Canaan's shore!

As the barley-winnower, holding with pain
Aloft in waiting his chaff and grain,

Joyfully welcomes the far-off breeze
Sounding the pine-tree's slender keys,
So he who had waited long to hear
The sound of the Spirit drawing near,
Like that which the son of Iddo heard
When the feet of angels the myrtles stirred,
Felt the answer of prayer, at last,
As over his church the afflatus passed,
Breaking its sleep as breezes break
To sun-bright ripples a stagnant lake.

At first a tremor of silent fear,
The creep of the flesh at danger near,
A vague foreboding and discontent,
Over the hearts of the people went.
All nature warned in sounds and signs:
The wind in the tops of the forest pines
In the name of the Highest called to prayer,
As the muezzin calls from the minaret stair.
Through ceiléd chambers of secret sin
Sudden and strong the light shone in;
A guilty sense of his neighbor's needs
Startled the man of title-deeds;

The trembling hand of the worldling shook
The dust of years from the Holy Book;
And the psalms of David, forgotten long,
Took the place of the scoffer's song.

The impulse spread like the outward course
Of waters moved by a central force:
The tide of spiritual life rolled down
From inland mountains to seaboard town.

Prepared and ready the altar stands
Waiting the prophet's outstretched hands
And prayer availing, to downward call
The fiery answer in view of all.
Hearts are like wax in the furnace, who
Shall mould, and shape, and cast them anew?
Lo! by the Merrimack WHITEFIELD stands
In the temple that never was made by hands,—
Curtains of azure, and crystal wall,
And dome of the sunshine over all!—
A homeless pilgrim, with dubious name
Blown about on the winds of fame;

Now as an angel of blessing classed,
And now as a mad enthusiast.
Called in his youth to sound and gauge
The moral lapse of his race and age,
And, sharp as truth, the contrast draw
Of human frailty and perfect law:
Possessed by the one dread thought that lent
Its goad to his fiery temperament,
Up and down the world he went,
A John the Baptist crying — Repent!

No perfect whole can our nature make;
Here or there the circle will break:
The orb of life as it takes the light
On one side leaves the other in night.
Never was saint so good and great
As to give no chance at St. Peter's gate
For the plea of the devil's advocate.
So, incomplete by his being's law,
The marvellous preacher had his flaw:
With step unequal, and lame with faults
His shade on the path of History halts.

Wisely and well said the Eastern bard:
Fear is easy, but love is hard,—
Easy to glow with the Santon's rage,
And walk on the Meccan pilgrimage;
But he is greatest and best who can
Worship Allah by loving man.

Thus he — to whom, in the painful stress
Of zeal on fire from its own excess,
Heaven seemed so vast and earth so small
That man was nothing, since God was all —
Forgot, as the best at times have done,
That the love of the Lord and of man are one.
Little to him whose feet unshod
The thorny path of the desert trod,
Careless of pain, so it led to God,
Seemed the hunger-pang and the poor man's wrong,
The weak ones trodden beneath the strong.
Should the worm be chooser? — the clay withstand
The shaping will of the potter's hand?

In the Indian fable Arjoon hears
The scorn of a god rebuke his fears:

"Spare thy pity!" Krishna saith:
"Not in thy sword is the power of death!
All is illusion, — loss but seems:
Pleasure and pain are only dreams:
Who deems he slayeth doth not kill;
Who counts as slain is living still.
Strike, nor fear thy blow is crime:
Nothing dies but the cheats of time:
Slain or slayer, small the odds
To each, immortal as Indra's gods!"

So by Savanna's banks of shade,
The stones of his mission the preacher laid
On the heart of the negro crushed and rent,
And made of his blood the wall's cement;
Bade the slave-ship speed from coast to coast
Fanned by the wings of the Holy Ghost;
And begged, for the love of Christ, the gold
Coined from the hearts in its groaning hold.
What could it matter, more or less
Of stripes, and hunger, and weariness?
Living or dying, bond or free,
What was time to eternity?

Alas for the preacher's cherished schemes!
Mission and church are now but dreams;
Nor prayer nor fasting availed the plan
To honor God through the wrong of man.
Of all his labors no trace remains
Save the bondman lifting his hands in chains.
The woof he wove in the righteous warp
Of freedom-loving Oglethorpe,
Clothes with curses the goodly land,
Changes its greenness and bloom to sand;
And a century's lapse reveals once more
The slave-ship stealing to Georgia's shore.
Father of Light! how blind is he
Who sprinkles the altar he rears to Thee
With the blood and tears of humanity!

He erred: Shall we count his gifts as naught?
Was the work of God in him unwrought?
The servant may through his deafness err,
And blind may be God's messenger;
But the errand is sure they go upon,—
The word is spoken, the deed is done.

Was the Hebrew temple less fair and good
That Solomon bowed to gods of wood?
For his tempted heart and wandering feet,
Were the songs of David less pure and sweet?
So in light and shadow the preacher went,
God's erring and human instrument;
And the hearts of the people where he passed
Swayed as the reeds sway in the blast.
Under the spell of a voice which took
In its compass the flow of Siloa's brook,
And the mystical chime of the bells of gold
On the ephod's hem of the priest of old. —
Now the roll of thunder, and now the awe
Of the trumpet heard in the Mount of Law.

A solemn fear on the listening crowd
Fell like the shadow of a cloud.
The sailor reeling from out the ships
Whose masts stood thick in the river slips
Felt the jest and the curse die on his lips.
Listened the fisherman rude and hard,
The calker rough from the builder's yard,

The man of the market left his load,
The teamster leaned on his bending goad,
The maiden, and youth beside her, felt
Their hearts in a closer union melt,
And saw the flowers of their love in bloom
Down the endless vistas of life to come.
Old age sat feebly brushing away
From his ears the scanty locks of gray;
And careless boyhood, living the free
Unconscious life of bird and tree,
Suddenly wakened to a sense
Of sin and its guilty consequence.
It was as if an angel's voice
Called the listeners up for their final choice;
As if a strong hand rent apart
The vails of sense from soul and heart,
Showing in light ineffable
The joys of heaven and woes of hell!
All about in the misty air
The hills seemed kneeling in silent prayer;
The rustle of leaves, the moaning sedge,
The water's lap on its gravelled edge,

The wailing pines, and, far and faint,
The wood-dove's note of sad complaint, —
To the solemn voice of the preacher lent
An undertone as of low lament:
And the rote of the sea from its sandy coast,
On the easterly wind, now heard, now lost,
Seemed the murmurous sound of the judgment host.

Yet wise men doubted, and good men wept,
As that storm of passion above them swept,
And, comet-like, adding flame to flame,
The priests of the new Evangel came, —
Davenport, flashing upon the crowd,
Charged like summer's electric cloud,
Now holding the listener still as death
With terrible warnings under breath,
Now shouting for joy, as if he viewed
The vision of Heaven's beatitude!
And Celtic Tennant, his long coat bound
Like a monk's with leathern girdle round,
Wild with the toss of unshorn hair,
And wringing of hands, and eyes aglare,

Groaning under the world's despair!
Grave pastors, grieving their flocks to lose,
Prophesied to the empty pews
That gourds would wither, and mushrooms die,
And noisiest fountains run soonest dry,
Like the spring that gushed in Newbury street,
Under the tramp of the earthquake's feet,
A silver shaft in the air and light,
For a single day, then lost in night,
Leaving only, its place to tell,
Sandy fissure and sulphurous smell.
With zeal wing-clipped and white heat cool,
Moved by the spirit in grooves of rule,
No longer harried, and cropped, and fleeced,
Flogged by sheriff and cursed by priest,
But by wiser councils left at ease
To settle quietly on his lees,
And, self-concentred, to count as done
The work which his fathers scarce begun,
In silent protest of letting alone,
The Quaker kept the way of his own, —
A non-conductor among the wires,
With coat of asbestos proof to fires.

And quite unable to mend his pace
To catch the falling manna of grace,
He hugged the closer his little store
Of faith, and silently prayed for more.
And vague of creed and barren of rite,
But holding, as in his Master's sight,
Act and thought to the inner light,
The round of his simple duties walked,
And strove to live what the others talked!

And who shall marvel if evil went
Step by step with the good intent,
And with love and meekness, side by side,
Lust of the flesh and spiritual pride?
That passionate longings and fancies vain
Set the heart on fire and crazed the brain? —
That over the holy oracles
Folly sported with cap and bells? —
That goodly women and learned men
Marvelling told with tongue and pen
How unweaned children chirped like birds
Texts of Scripture and solemn words,

Like the infant seers of the rocky glens
In the Puy de Dome of wild Cevennes:
Or baby Lamas who pray and preach
From Tartar cradles in Buddha's speech!

In the war which Truth or Freedom wages
With impious fraud and the wrong of ages,
Hate and malice and self-love mar
The notes of triumph with painful jar,
And the helping angels turn aside
Their sorrowing faces the shame to hide.
Never on custom's oiléd grooves
The world to a higher level moves,
But grates and grinds with friction hard
On granite boulder and flinty shard.
The heart must bleed before it feels,
The pool be troubled before it heals;
Ever by losses the right must gain,
Every good have its birth of pain;
The active Virtues blush to find
The Vices wearing their badge behind,
And Graces and Charities feel the fire
Wherein the sins of the age expire;

The fiend still rends as of old he rent
The tortured body from which he went.

But Time tests all. In the overdrift
And flow of the Nile, with its annual gift,
Who cares for the Hadji's relics sunk?
Who thinks of the drowned-out Coptic monk?
The tide that loosens the temple's stones,
And scatters the sacred ibis bones,
Drives away from the valley-land
That Arab robber, the wandering sand,
Moistens the fields that know no rain,
Fringes the desert with belts of grain,
And bread to the sower brings again.
So the flood of emotion deep and strong
Troubled the land as it swept along,
But left a result of holier lives,
Tenderer mothers and worthier wives.
The husband and father whose children fled
And sad wife wept when his drunken tread
Frightened peace from his roof-tree's shade,
And a rock of offence his hearthstone made,

In a strength that was not his own, began
To rise from the brute's to the plane of man.
Old friends embraced, long held apart
By evil counsel and pride of heart;
And penitence saw through misty tears,
In the bow of hope on its cloud of fears,
The promise of Heaven's eternal years, —
The peace of God for the world's annoy, —
Beauty for ashes, and oil of joy!

Under the church of Federal-street,
Under the tread of its Sabbath feet,
Walled about by its basement stones,
Lie the marvellous preacher's bones.
No saintly honors to them are shown,
No sign nor miracle have they known;
But he who passes the ancient church
Stops in the shade of its belfry-porch,
And ponders the wonderful life of him
Who lies at rest in that charnel dim.
Long shall the traveller strain his eye
From the railroad car, as it plunges by,

And the vanishing town behind him search
For the slender spire of the Whitefield Church;
And feel for one moment the ghosts of trade,
And fashion, and folly, and pleasure laid,
By the thought of that life of pure intent,
That voice of warning yet eloquent,
Of one on the errands of angels sent.
And if where he labored the flood of sin
Like a tide from the harbor-bar sets in,
And over a life of time and sense
The church-spires lift their vain defence,
As if to scatter the bolts of God
With the points of Calvin's thunder-rod,—
Still, as the gem of its civic crown,
Precious beyond the world's renown,
His memory hallows the ancient town!

THE QUAKER ALUMNI.*

From the well-springs of Hudson, the sea-cliffs of
    Maine,
Grave men, sober matrons, you gather again;
And, with hearts warmer grown as your heads grow
    more cool,
Play over the old game of going to school.

All your strifes and vexations, your whims and
    complaints,
(You were not saints yourselves, if the children of
    saints!)
All your petty self-seekings and rivalries done,
Round the dear Alma Mater your hearts beat as one!

How widely soe'er you have strayed from the fold,
Though your "thee" has grown "you," and your
    drab blue and gold,

---

* Read at the Friends' School Anniversary, Providence, R. I., 6th mo., 1860.

To the old friendly speech and the garb's sober form,
Like the heart of Argyle to the tartan, you warm.

But, the first greetings over, you glance round the
    hall;
Your hearts call the roll, but they answer not all:
Through the turf green above them the dead cannot
    hear;
Name by name, in the silence, falls sad as a tear!

In love, let us trust, they were summoned so soon
From the morning of life, while we toil through its
    noon;
They were frail like ourselves, they had needs like
    our own,
And they rest as we rest in God's mercy alone.

Unchanged by our changes of spirit and frame,
Past, now, and henceforward the Lord is the same:
Though we sink in the darkness, his arms break our
    fall,
And in death as in life he is Father of all!

We are older: our footsteps, so light in the play
Of the far-away schooltime, move slower to-day; —
Here a beard touched with frost, there a bald, shining crown,
And beneath the cap's border gray mingles with brown.

But faith should be cheerful, and trust should be glad,
And our follies and sins, not our years, make us sad.
Should the heart closer shut as the bonnet grows prim,
And the face grow in length as the hat grows in brim?

Life is brief, duty grave; but, with rain-folded wings,
Of yesterday's sunshine the grateful heart sings;
And we, of all others, have reason to pay
The tribute of thanks, and rejoice on our way,

For the counsels that turned from the follies of youth;
For the beauty of patience, the whiteness of truth;

For the wounds of rebuke, when love tempered its
    edge;
For the household's restraint, and the discipline's
    hedge;

For the lessons of kindness vouchsafed to the least
Of the creatures of God, whether human or beast,
Bringing hope to the poor, lending strength to the
    frail
In the lanes of the city, the slave-hut, and jail:

For a womanhood higher and holier, by all
Her knowledge of good, than was Eve ere her fall, —
Whose task-work of duty moves lightly as play,
Serene as the moonlight and warm as the day;

And, yet more, for the faith which embraces the
    whole,
Of the creeds of the ages the life and the soul,
Wherein letter and spirit the same channel run,
And man has not severed what God has made one!

For a sense of the Goodness revealed everywhere,
As sunshine impartial, and free as the air;
For a trust in humanity, Heathen or Jew,
And a hope for all darkness The Light shineth through.

Who scoffs at our birthright? — the words of the seers,
And the songs of the bards in the twilight of years.
All the fore-gleams of wisdom in santon and sage,
In prophet and priest, are our true heritage.

The Word which the reason of Plato discerned;
The truth, as whose symbol the Mithra-fire burned;
The soul of the world which the Stoic but guessed,
In the Light Universal the Quaker confessed!

No honors of war to our worthies belong;
Their plain stem of life never flowered into song;
But the fountains they opened still gush by the way,
And the world for their healing is better to-day.

He who lies where the minster's groined arches
    curve down
To the tomb-crowded transept of England's renown,
The glorious essayist, by genius enthroned,
Whose pen as a sceptre the Muses all owned,—

Who through the world's pantheon walked in his
    pride,
Setting new statues up, thrusting old ones aside,
And in fiction the pencils of history dipped,
To gild o'er or blacken each saint in his crypt,—

How vainly he labored to sully with blame
The white bust of Penn, in the niche of his fame!
Self-will is self-wounding, perversity blind:
On himself fell the stain for the Quaker designed!

For the sake of his true-hearted father before him;
For the sake of the dear Quaker mother that bore him;
For the sake of his gifts, and the works that outlive
    him,
And his brave words for freedom, we freely forgive
    him!

There are those who take note that our numbers are
    small, —
New Gibbons who write our decline and our fall;
But the Lord of the seed-field takes care of his own,
And the world shall yet reap what our sowers have
    sown.

The last of the sect to his fathers may go,
Leaving only his coat for some Barnum to show;
But the truth will outlive him, and broaden with years,
Till the false dies away, and the wrong disappears.

Nothing fails of its end. Out of sight sinks the stone,
In the deep sea of time, but the circles sweep on,
Till the low-rippled murmurs along the shores run,
And the dark and dead waters leap glad in the sun.

Meanwhile shall we learn, in our ease, to forget
To the martyrs of Truth and of Freedom our debt? —
Hide their words out of sight, like the garb that they
    wore,
And for Barclay's Apology offer one more?

Shall we fawn round the priestcraft that glutted the
    shears,
And festooned the stocks with our grandfathers'
    ears? —
Talk of Woolman's unsoundness? — count Penn
    heterodox?
And take Cotton Mather in place of George Fox? —

Make our preachers war-chaplains? — quote Scrip-
    ture to take
The hunted slave back, for Onesimus' sake? —
Go to burning church-candles, and chanting in choir,
And on the old meeting-house stick up a spire?

No! the old paths we'll keep until better are shown,
Credit good where we find it, abroad or our own;
And while "Lo here" and "Lo there" the multitude
    call,
Be true to ourselves, and do justice to all.

The good round about us we need not refuse,
Nor talk of our Zion as if we were Jews;

But why shirk the badge which our fathers have worn,
Or beg the world's pardon for having been born?

We need not pray over the Pharisee's prayer,
Nor claim that our wisdom is Benjamin's share.
Truth to us and to others is equal and one:
Shall we bottle the free air, or hoard up the sun?

Well know we our birthright may serve but to show
How the meanest of weeds in the richest soil grow;
But we need not disparage the good which we hold:
Though the vessels be earthen, the treasure is gold!

Enough and too much of the sect and the name.
What matters our label, so truth be our aim?
The creed may be wrong, but the life may be true,
And hearts beat the same under drab coats or blue.

So the man *be* a man, let him worship at will,
In Jerusalem's courts, or on Gerizim's hill.

When she makes up her jewels, what cares the good town
For the Baptist of WAYLAND, the Quaker of BROWN?

And this green, favored island, so fresh and sea-blown.
When she counts up the worthies her annals have known,
Never waits for the pitiful gaugers of sect
To measure her love, and mete out her respect.

Three shades at this moment seem walking her strand,
Each with head halo-crowned, and with palms in his hand, —
Wise Berkeley, grave Hopkins, and, smiling serene
On prelate and puritan, Channing is seen.

One holy name bearing, no longer they need
Credentials of party, and pass-words of creed:
The new song they sing hath a three-fold accord,
And they own one baptism, one faith, and one Lord!

But the golden sands run out: Occasions like these
Glide swift into shadow, like sails on the seas:
While we sport with the mosses and pebbles ashore,
They lessen and fade, and we see them no more.

Forgive me, dear friends, if my vagrant thoughts seem
Like a school-boy's who idles and plays with his theme.
Forgive the light measure whose changes display
The sunshine and rain of our brief April day.

There are moments in life when the lip and the eye
Try the question of whether to smile or to cry;
And scenes and reunions that prompt like our own
The tender in feeling, the playful in tone.

I, who never sat down with the boys and the girls
At the feet of your Slocums, and Cartlands, and Earles, —
By courtesy only permitted to lay
On your festival's altar my poor gift, to day, —

I would joy in your joy: let me have a friend's part
In the warmth of your welcome of hand and of
heart,—
On your play-ground of boyhood unbend the brow's
care,
And shift the old burdens our shoulders must bear

Long live the good School! giving out year by year
Recruits to true manhood, and womanhood dear:
Brave boys, modest maidens, in beauty sent forth,
The living epistles and proof of its worth!

In and out let the young life as steadily flow
As in broad Narraganset the tides come and go;
And its sons and its daughters in prairie and town
Remember its honor, and guard its renown.

Not vainly the gift of its founder was made;
Not prayerless the stones of its corner were laid:
The blessing of Him whom in secret they sought
Has owned the good work which the fathers have
wrought.

To Him be the glory forever! — We bear
To the Lord of the Harvest our wheat with the tare.
What we lack in our work may He find in our will,
And winnow in mercy our good from the ill!

BROWN OF OSSAWATOMIE.

John Brown of Ossawatomie spake on his dying day:
"I will not have to shrive my soul a priest in Slavery's pay.
But let some poor slave-mother whom I have striven to free,
With her children from the gallows-stair put up a prayer for me!"

John Brown of Ossawatomie, they led him out to die;
And lo! a poor slave-mother with her little child pressed nigh.
Then the bold, blue eye grew tender, and the old harsh face grew mild,
As he stooped between the jeering ranks and kissed the negro's child!

The shadows of his stormy life that moment fell
    apart;
And they who blamed the bloody hand forgave the
    loving heart.
That kiss from all its guilty means redeemed the
    good intent,
And round the grisly fighter's hair the martyr's
    aureole bent!

Perish with him the folly that seeks through evil
    good!
Long live the generous purpose unstained with
    human blood!
Not the raid of midnight terror, but the thought
    which underlies;
Not the borderer's pride of daring, but the Chris-
    tian's sacrifice.

Never more may yon Blue Ridges the Northern rifle
    hear,
Nor see the light of blazing homes flash on the
    negro's spear.

But let the free-winged angel Truth their guarded
    passes scale,
To teach that right is more than might, and justice
    more than mail!

So vainly shall Virginia set her battle in array;
In vain her trampling squadrons knead the winter
    snow with clay.
She may strike the pouncing eagle, but she dares
    not harm the dove:
And every gate she bars to Hate shall open wide to
    Love!

FROM PERUGIA.

"The thing which has the most dissevered the people from the Pope, the *unforgivable* thing, — the breaking point between him and them, — has been the encouragement and promotion he gave to the officer under whom were executed the slaughters of Perugia. *That* made the breaking point in many honest hearts that had clung to him before."

HARRIET BEECHER STOWE'S "LETTERS FROM ITALY."

THE tall, sallow guardsmen their horse-tails have spread,
Flaming out in their violet, yellow, and red;
And behind go the lackeys in crimson and buff,
And the chamberlains gorgeous in velvet and ruff;
Next, in red-legged pomp, come the cardinals forth,
Each a lord of the church and a prince of the earth.

What's this squeak of the fife, and this batter of drum?
Lo! the Swiss of the Church from Perugia come,—
The militant angels, whose sabres drive home

To the hearts of the malcontents, cursed and abhorred
The good Father's missives, and "Thus saith the Lord!"
And lend to his logic the point of the sword!

O maids of Etruria, gazing forlorn
O'er dark Thrasymenus, dishevelled and torn!
O fathers, who pluck at your gray beards for shame!
O mothers, struck dumb by a woe without name!
Well ye know how the Holy Church hireling behaves,
And his tender compassion of prisons and graves!

There they stand, the hired stabbers, the bloodstains yet fresh,
That splashed like red wine from the vintage of flesh, —
Grim instruments, careless as pincers and rack
How the joints tear apart, and the strained sinews crack;

But the hate that glares on them is sharp as their
    swords,
And the sneer and the scowl print the air with
    fierce words!

Off with hats, down with knees, shout your vivas
    like mad!
Here's the Pope in his holiday righteousness clad,
From shorn crown to toe-nail, kiss-worn to the
    quick,
Of sainthood in purple the pattern and pick,
Who the *role* of the priest and the soldier unites,
And praying like Aaron, like Joshua fights!

Is this Pio Nono the gracious, for whom
We sang our hosannas and lighted all Rome;
With whose advent we dreamed the new era began
When the priest should be human, the monk be a
    man?
Ah, the wolf's with the sheep, and the fox with the
    fowl,
When freedom we trust to the crozier and cowl!

Stand aside, men of Rome! Here's a hangman-faced
    Swiss —
(A blessing for him surely can't go amiss) —
Would kneel down the sanctified slipper to kiss.
Short shrift will suffice him — he's blest beyond
    doubt;
But there's blood on his hands which would scarcely
    wash out,
Though Peter himself held the baptismal spout!

Make way for the next! Here's another sweet
    son!
What's this mastiff-jawed rascal in epaulettes done?
He did, whispers rumor (its truth God forbid!)
At Perugia what Herod at Bethlehem did.
And the mothers? — Don't name them! — these
    humors of war
They who keep him in service must pardon him
    for.

Hist! here's the arch-knave in a cardinal's hat,
With the heart of a wolf, and the stealth of a cat

(As if Judas and Herod together were rolled),
Who keeps, all as one, the Pope's conscience and
gold,
Mounts guard on the altar, and pilfers from thence,
And flatters St. Peter while stealing his pence!

Who doubts Antonelli? Have miracles ceased
When robbers say mass, and Barabbas is priest?
When the Church eats and drinks, at its mystical
board,
The true flesh and blood carved and shed by its
sword,
When its martyr, unsinged, claps the crown on his
head,
And roasts, as his proxy, his neighbor instead!

There! the bells jow and jangle the same blessed
way
That they did when they rang for Bartholomew's day.
Hark! the tallow-faced monsters, nor women nor
boys,
Vex the air with a shrill, sexless horror of noise.

Te Deum laudamus! — All round without stint
The incense-pot swings with a taint of blood in 't!

And now for the blessing! Of little account,
You know, is the old one they heard on the Mount.
Its giver was landless, his raiment was poor,
No jewelled tiara his fishermen wore :
No incense, no lackeys, no riches, no home,
No Swiss guards! — We order things better at
 Rome.

So bless us the strong hand, and curse us the weak:
Let Austria's vulture have food for her beak ;
Let the wolf-whelp of Naples play Bomba again,
With his death-cap of silence, and halter, and chain ;
Put reason, and justice, and truth under ban ;
For the sin unforgiven is freedom for man!

FOR AN AUTUMN FESTIVAL.

The Persian's flowery gifts, the shrine
    Of fruitful Ceres, charm no more;
The woven wreaths of oak and pine
    Are dust along the Isthmian shore.

But beauty hath its homage still,
    And nature holds us still in debt;
And woman's grace and household skill,
    And manhood's toil, are honored yet.

And we, to-day, amidst our flowers
    And fruits, have come to own again
The blessing of the summer hours,
    The early and the latter rain;

To see our Father's hand once more
    Reverse for us the plenteous horn
Of autumn, filled and running o'er
    With fruit, and flower, and golden corn!

FOR AN AUTUMN FESTIVAL.

Once more the liberal year laughs out
    O'er richer stores than gems or gold;
Once more with harvest-song and shout
    Is Nature's bloodless triumph told.

Our common mother rests and sings,
    Like Ruth, among her garnered sheaves;
Her lap is full of goodly things,
    Her brow is bright with autumn leaves.

O, favors every year made new!
    O, gifts with rain and sunshine sent!
The bounty overruns our due,
    The fullness shames our discontent.

We shut our eyes, the flowers bloom on;
    We murmur, but the corn-ears fill;
We choose the shadow, but the sun
    That casts it shines behind us still

God gives us with our rugged soil
    The power to make it Eden-fair,
And richer fruits to crown our toil
    Than summer-wedded islands bear.

Who murmurs at his lot to-day?
    Who scorns his native fruit and bloom?
Or sighs for dainties far away,
    Beside the bounteous board of home?

Thank Heaven, instead, that Freedom's arm
    Can change a rocky soil to gold, —
That brave and generous lives can warm
    A clime with northern ices cold.

And let these altars wreathed with flowers
    And piled with fruits awake again
Thanksgiving for the golden hours,
    The early and the latter rain!

www.ingramcontent.com/pod-product-compliance
Lightning Source LLC
Chambersburg PA
CBHW020914230426
43666CB00008B/1451